THE HOLY COMMUNION
An Exposition of the Prayer Book Service

THE PRAYER BOOK COMMENTARIES
EDITED BY FRANK COLQUHOUN

THE HOLY COMMUNION

An Exposition of
the Prayer Book Service

by

MARTIN PARSONS

London
HODDER AND STOUGHTON

PREFACE

THIS book is one of a series of *Prayer Book Commentaries*. I have received valued help from the General Editor, but I must take full responsibility for the views I have expressed, and for the many weaknesses of which I am only too conscious.

I have not written for the clergy, or indeed for any other scholars or students of liturgy. For them there are the more learned books. I have tried to keep in mind the ordinary worshipper, whose devotion might be deepened by increased knowledge.

My own indebtedness to others is obvious. Except where I have quoted directly, I have not wittingly "ploughed with another man's heifer", but so many streams have contributed to my own experience that I cannot say that I may not unconsciously have borrowed words as well as ideas. But even more than to books, sermons, lectures and conversations, I owe a debt to the congregations with whom I have shared in the Holy Communion. Anything I have written that may be of any value has grown out of this corporate life of the Church in its local setting.

I dedicate this book to the congregation I now serve at Emmanuel, Northwood, and desire any royalties that may accrue from its sale to be paid to that parish.

My prayer is that, through the reading of what follows, some may be led to a fuller understanding of the Lord's Supper and consequently a closer walk with God. I hope also that some may want to pursue the study of the Book of Common Prayer, with all its rich treasures. My one desire is to edify, and if in places I have expressed views which may be controversial, I

trust that readers will accept my assurance that I have tried
to do so "in love".

M. P.

Northwood.

All quotations from the Bible are taken from the Revised
Standard Version, unless otherwise stated.

CONTENTS

THE HOLY COMMUNION
An Exposition of the Prayer Book Service

CHAPTER I

THE BREAKING OF BREAD

THE earliest Christian converts continued steadfastly in the apostles' teaching and fellowship, in the breaking of bread and the prayers (Acts 2:42). As the Revised Standard Version translates it, "they devoted themselves" to these things. A constant danger in the life of the Church is that Christians will not continue in the race, not devote themselves to their discipleship. The four things mentioned in the Acts as characteristic of those early days are all essential: apostolic teaching, fellowship, and prayer, no less than the breaking of bread. But it is with the breaking of bread that we are concerned in this book. What did the first Christians understand when they continued steadfastly in the breaking of bread? The answer to that question will help us to grasp the significance of the Holy Communion for us today.

THE CENTRALITY OF THE CROSS

First, they bore witness that their faith was centred in Christ crucified. "The Lord Jesus on the night when he was betrayed took bread, and when he had given thanks, he broke it, and said, 'This is my body which is for you. Do this in remembrance of me.' In the same way also the cup, after supper, saying, 'This cup is the new covenant in my blood. Do this, as often as you drink it, in remembrance of me.' For as often as you eat this bread and drink the cup, you proclaim the Lord's death until he comes" (1 Cor. 11:23-26). Because so much depends upon the Cross, this Sacrament was given to be *a perpetual memory of that his precious death, until his coming again.*

There will never be any continuance in the Christian life if we get away from the fact of our redemption through the death of Christ. There is far more meaning in the Cross than we shall ever be able to understand. Theories of the atonement may help us to grasp little bits of the truth of this great subject. But there is a grand simplicity about the *fact* of redemption which we must never lose. The heart of the gospel is: "While we were yet sinners Christ died for us" (Rom. 5:8). The basis of a Christian experience is to be able to say: "The Son of God, who loved me and gave himself for me" (Gal. 2:20).

The moment a Christian begins to think he has outgrown the simple gospel, he is in a state of spiritual peril. Charles Augustus Toplady thought he detected this danger in the Methodist emphasis on holiness of life. To him it seemed that they were relying on their spiritual condition to commend them to God, and this he saw as a denial of the efficacy of the Cross alone for salvation. Subsequent generations have seen that the Wesleys were only teaching another side of the same truth. Nevertheless it was a stroke of genius—or inspiration—which made Toplady call his *Rock of Ages* "a living and dying prayer for the holiest believer in the world". It could certainly be a prayer for the greatest sinner to use; but Toplady wrote it to drive home the fact that, however far a Christian may progress in holiness, he still has nothing to plead but the fact of the Cross. In life and in death the holiest saint must still pray:

> Nothing in my hand I bring,
> Simply to thy cross I cling.

This is virtually what we say when we come to the Lord's Table. We are brought again to the Cross, and casting away all trust in our own supposed goodness, we throw ourselves wholly upon what Christ has done for us. It is all made real to us in the breaking of bread. We see afresh what God has done for our salvation. Our feelings are quite unimportant. Even our faith is secondary. God's great act of redemption stands out for our acceptance.

It is for this very reason, among others, that every Christian, like the first disciples, must continue steadfastly in the breaking of bread throughout the whole of life. When moods change and feelings fail, the objectivity of the Holy Communion remains.

FEEDING ON CHRIST

Secondly, the early Christians, by their steadfast continuance in the breaking of bread, confessed that all their spiritual sustenance was in Christ. "Take, eat; this is my body" (Matt. 26:26). The Lord's Supper puts into a very simple action the teaching which our Lord gave about himself as the Bread of Life. The miracle of the feeding of the five thousand gave rise, in the account in St. John 6, to the discourse about the true bread from heaven. The climax, which made even some of his disciples depart from him, was when he spoke of the absolute necessity of eating his flesh and drinking his blood. "For my flesh is food indeed, and my blood is drink indeed" (John 6:55). This Eastern and pictorial language speaks of partaking in our inmost being of the very life of Christ, as that life was poured out for us on the Cross.

Spiritual life begins at the Cross. It is there that we are reconciled to God. And the life that is given as God's free gift is nourished and strengthened by feeding upon Christ. There are of course many ways in which we feed on him. Bible reading, prayer, meditation, fellowship are all means by which we receive grace. But the connection between the language of St. John 6 and the symbolism of the Lord's Supper leads us to the belief that here is a very special way in which our spiritual life is to be nourished. Partaking of the Holy Communion reminds us that we have need of strength which only Christ can give. The benefit we receive is "the strengthening and refreshing of our souls by the Body and Blood of Christ, as our bodies are by the Bread and Wine" (Catechism). We feed on him in our hearts by faith.

It is essential for all who would continue in the Christian life, not only to know the reality of reconciliation through the Cross, but also to find in Christ their sanctification and strength. It is vital to remember that sanctification is not a theory or an experience, but Christ himself. "He is the source of your life in Christ Jesus, whom God made our wisdom, our righteousness and sanctification and redemption" (1 Cor. 1:30). It is when Christ really dwells in our hearts by faith that we are rooted and grounded in love, and are made strong to apprehend the love of God. (See Eph. 3:17-19).

Precisely for the reason that at the Lord's Supper we feed on Christ in our hearts by faith, we need to continue steadfastly in the breaking of bread throughout our whole lives.

THE FELLOWSHIP MEAL

Thirdly, as they continued in the breaking of bread, they showed their one-ness in Christ. "The cup of blessing which we bless, is it not a participation in the body of Christ? The bread which we break is it not a participation in the body of Christ? Because there is one loaf, we who are many are one body, for we all partake of the same loaf" (1 Cor. 10:16-17). Joint participation in the Sacrament was a visible expression of their fellowship, and a means of deepening it.

Fellowship is a word which is not only in danger of being overdone, but is also much misunderstood. It can be taken to mean little more than the friendship of people who happen to like each other and share the same interests. There is nothing particularly Christian about this. A voluntary association of people with a common purpose ought to be able to join its members together in a happy unity. Anyone who does not like the particular group, or who loses interest in the object of its existence, can easily resign without upsetting the working of the whole.

Christian fellowship is something totally different. We do not join the Church or resign from it according to our whim. We are in the Church from the moment we are in Christ. Our fellow members are not those whom we have chosen because

we like them. They may be people of quite another background
and with different interests. They may be of some other race
and language. The one thing we all have in common—and it
does not seem a very promising basis for fellowship—is that
we are all sinners. But we are sinners who are willing to own
up to it, and have sought and found mercy in Christ. The experience of a new birth has brought us into the Church, which
is his Body.

The infinite variety of membership in the Christian Church
cannot be better described than in St. Paul's metaphor of the
body. "For just as the body is one and has many members, and
all the members of the body, though many, are one body, so it
is with Christ. For by one Spirit we were all baptized into one
body—Jews or Greeks, slaves or free—and all were made to
drink of one Spirit" (1 Cor. 12:12, 13). Anything like jealousy
or a feeling of being unwanted would be as absurd as for one
member of the human body to say to another, "I have no need
of you" (1 Cor. 12:21).

It is this unity in diversity which the first Christians expressed as they met together for the breaking of bread. They
ate of the one loaf and drank of the one cup. They were one
because they were partaking together of the one Christ. The
breaking of bread is never an individual matter. "I made my
communion" is, to say the least, an incomplete account of what
happens. It is not merely a social matter either. Communicants
are something more than the aggregate of worshippers at a particular service. It is a *corporate* matter. The Church is showing
what it really is, the Body of Christ.

That is why the ideal Communion Service is one at which
the whole company of believers in a given place comes together
at one time for the breaking of bread. The trend in this direction in the Church of England is to be welcomed. However
necessary it may be in practice to hold a number of smaller services, or a "corporate" Communion for a section of the parish,
it is not really a complete act of fellowship. Any barrier at the
Lord's Table, whatever the motive or purpose, is a contradiction

B

of New Testament principles. That is why the continuance of disunity among Christians will always be felt most acutely at the Lord's Supper.

THANKSGIVING

Fourthly, as the early Christians continued steadfastly in the breaking of bread they gave expression to their sense of thankfulness. This was true to the original institution in the upper room in which our Lord *took the cup, and when he had given thanks, he gave it to them.* Indeed thanksgiving was characteristic of the life of the infant Church. "Day by day, attending the temple together and breaking bread in their homes, they partook of food with glad and generous hearts, praising God and having favour with all the people" (Acts 2:46, 47). No one can be made more aware of the benefits of Christ's passion without thankfully responding to him "in full and glad surrender".

The bread is broken because Christ's body was broken on the Cross. But we remember that the Church is also his Body. The one loaf speaks of its unity : its breaking speaks of its sacrifice. We offer a sacrifice of praise and thanksgiving, not only with our lips but in our lives. We cannot really partake of Christ crucified and risen unless we are willing to go the way of the Cross. "I have been crucified with Christ; it is no longer I who live, but Christ who lives in me" (Gal. 2:20). Those words of St. Paul are as true for the Church as they are for an individual Christian.

The breaking process is hard and costly, but Christian experience all down the centuries shows that it is the way of fruitfulness for us, as it was for our Master. "Unless a grain of wheat falls into the earth and dies, it remains alone; but if it dies, it bears much fruit" (John 12:24). This is the offering which God asks of us : *ourselves, our souls and bodies.* We have nothing worthy to offer in ourselves, but only in the name of him who made the one perfect sacrifice of himself. Yet in response to the love of God in Christ we can do no less than offer him our redeemed lives. This is our sacrifice of praise and thanksgiving.

Four things, then, were in the minds of the early Christians as they continued in the breaking of bread, and each corresponds with a term we use to describe the Sacrament. The centrality of the Cross brings to mind the word "Remembrance" which occurs particularly in the Exhortations in the Prayer Book. Feeding upon Christ links up naturally with the term "the Lord's Supper", which is used in the title of the service. Fellowship is another word for Communion, and reminds us that we very often speak of "the Holy Communion". Our offering of praise may be described as "the Eucharist", which is simply the Greek for thanksgiving. No one term can convey all the truth about the rich Banquet our Lord has provided for us.

CHAPTER 2

WHO MAY COME?

So many as intend to be partakers of the Holy Communion shall signify their names to the Curate, at least some time the day before. This rubric at the beginning of the Prayer Book service is seldom now observed. When it was first inserted parishes were smaller so that the "Curate" (i.e. the Minister who had the "cure" of souls in that place) knew all his people intimately, and the Holy Communion was celebrated less frequently than today. It was reasonable that the number of intending communicants should be known, so that sufficient bread and wine should be provided. More important, it gave the opportunity to the pastor to ensure that the people were preparing themselves adequately. It is interesting to observe that in the first English Prayer Book (1549) it was permitted to give notice of one's intention to partake either before or after Morning Prayer, though "overnight" was given as a first preference. The change to *at least some time the day before* in our present Prayer Book (1662) indicates an even greater emphasis on preparation.

One of the results of giving notice would be that the Curate could warn any *open and notorious evil liver*, or any parishioners *betwixt whom he perceiveth malice and hatred to reign*, not to come to the Lord's Table until there had been repentance and restitution. The directions given in the second and third rubrics are intended to lay down principles. It is open scandals which are in mind, not the sins of thought, word and deed of which we all need to repent. All sin is grievous, but where there is true repentance there is full forgiveness. The rubric speaks of those sins where it is quite clear to everybody that the sinner is not penitent.

Apart from this necessary precaution, the Church does not attempt to "fence" the Table. The rubric at the end of the Confirmation Service is not really an exception to this rule, i.e. the rubric which says, "And there shall none be admitted to the Holy Communion, until such time as he be confirmed, or be ready and desirous to be confirmed." This is surely because one who has not been confirmed has not yet openly and officially declared himself a Christian. He has been baptized as an infant, but the confession of faith was then made on his behalf by others. Until there has been that personal decision for Christ and commitment to him which is asked for at Confirmation, the baptized churchman has not yet accepted the implications of his Baptism. Holy Communion is not for those who have held back from committing themselves to the Saviour.

This is very different from saying that it is only for those who are "worthy" or "good enough". This is an error which is met with more often than many people realise. It may take the form of being afraid to come because of a sense of sin. Or it may be a criticism of someone else for coming, because he or she is not a perfect Christian. No one is fit to come. All we can bring is our need. If anyone thought he was "good enough" that would be a sure sign that he had not begun to understand the Christian message. All who desire to be on Christ's side, who want to turn afresh to him and put all their confidence in his saving grace, may come humbly and penitently to the Lord's Table. There is no other way to come.

We *ought* to come. To begin with, it is a question of obedience. It is very difficult to understand how some professing Christians feel they can neglect what Christ has commanded. When the Duke of Wellington heard some officers discussing foreign missions and suggesting that they were not necessary, he simply asked: "What are your marching orders?" The same might be said to those who neglect the Holy Communion. It has been commanded. Obedience, duty, obligation should be motive enough to make every Christian a faithful communicant.

Obviously there are other motives too. Holy Communion is a means of grace which we cannot ignore without grievous loss to our spiritual life. That is not to say that it is a different *kind* of grace which we receive at the Lord's Table. Indeed we ought never to think of grace as anything other than a renewed personal relationship with our Lord. But grace is given by various means, and we need them all: private prayer no less than public worship, Christian fellowship no less than Bible study. And the Lord's Supper is a divinely appointed means by which we are renewed in faith, in love, in communion. We neglect it at our peril.

HOW OFTEN?

We have already seen that in the earliest days of the Church the whole Christian Family met together for the breaking of bread at least every Lord's Day. The compilers of our Prayer Book faced a very different situation. In the pre-Reformation Church, while all attended Mass every Sunday, the Priest alone communicated. The Fourth Lateran Council, in 1215, had laid it down that all should receive Communion at least once a year, and that became the normal practice. So, when the Reformers provided *that every Parishioner shall communicate at the least three times in the year, of which Easter to be one,* they were moving in the direction of more frequent Communion.

Times of spiritual awakening have always had the effect of sending people back to the Lord's Table. While the men of the Oxford Movement made much of the Holy Communion, they were by no means alone in this. The Wesley Revival had its strong sacramental emphasis, and the Church Evangelicals saw their churches crowded with devout communicants. It was to meet this demand that in a number of evangelical churches Communion Services began to be held at the novel hour of 8 a.m. The practice has for many years persisted in almost all churches, but it is not necessarily the best time in our present circumstances.

It is a matter of great thankfulness that in many quarters there is a return to the primitive ideal of the whole Christian Family in a parish coming *together* to the Lord's Table. In some churches this Family Service or Parish Communion is held every Sunday, in others less frequently. The time of day at which such a service takes place is secondary; what is really important is that all Christian people should be encouraged to come regularly, and come together. Whether this is best accomplished with a Celebration at 9.30 in the morning, or as the principal service in the evening, or at any other time, will vary with the circumstances of each parish.

The prejudice which once existed against evening Communion is happily breaking down. The Sacrament was of course instituted after supper, and was celebrated in the evening in some places as late as the fifth century. If the chief objection to the practice is that it makes fasting Communion impossible, the same applies to a Celebration at a late morning hour. We should not wish to hinder anyone from fasting before Communion if it is found to be a helpful discipline, making for greater spiritual alertness. In many instances, however, it has exactly the opposite effect, and the Prayer Book is wisely silent on the subject. It is far more concerned with the preparation of the heart. We shall see how this is emphasised in the Exhortations which, to our loss, are now so seldom read.

Provided there is adequate preparation on each occasion, communicants should be encouraged to come to the Lord's Table as often as possible. The only responsible way for a Christian to act in this matter is to make a rule of life which will include a decision about the frequency of Communion. Those who say they will come "when they feel like it" will very soon find how often they do *not* feel like it. Such times are probably the occasions when they all the more need to come. Let there be a definite rule which will be unfailingly kept. Perhaps at the end of a year the rule might be reviewed, and if necessary revised to meet a more deeply felt need.

THE HOLY TABLE

When we come to church for the Holy Communion, we find the Holy Table with a fair white linen cloth upon it. It is important that attention should be given to such details. We are coming to the King's Feast. Everything must be the best that we can provide, spotless and beautiful. If the rubric were followed, the Table might either be in the body of the church, or in the chancel. Its removal into the nave for the Communion was in keeping with the Reformation principle of emphasising the communion of the people. This would be particularly important where there was a chancel screen which partly shut off the congregation from the chancel. But a century or so after the Reformation we find the Holy Table left in its position against the east wall of the chancel. Moreover, a Canon of 1640 enacted that it should be railed in, as unfortunately there had been cases of irreverence, even using the Table as a hat stand. The modern tendency to have the Table standing away from the wall, with the rail encircling it, has much to commend it.

The rubric concludes with the direction to *the Priest standing at the north side of the Table* to begin the service. It is commonly said that the position at the north side was only meant to apply when the Table stood "long ways on" in the body of the church. But the rubric remained unchanged even after the Table had been moved back to the Altar-wise position. Those, therefore, who stand at the north side (as is universally done in the Church of Ireland) would seem to be following the intentions of the Reformers. In the celebrated Lambeth Judgment of 1890, the Archbishop of Canterbury decided that the eastward position was also legal, provided the manual acts in the Prayer of Consecration were made visible to the people. It may be that, in a future revision of the Prayer Book, the westward position will be recommended, i.e. the celebrant standing behind the Table facing the people. This would be a return to primitive custom.

Inasmuch as the outward accompaniments of worship are

often symbolic of doctrine, they are not unimportant. It does matter whether true doctrine is being expressed in our ceremonies. Nevertheless, it is possible to be meticulously careful about forms, and to miss the inner meaning and spirit. The simple dignity and utter reverence of a celebration of Holy Communion, in accordance with Prayer Book directions, can be the greatest help to spiritual worship, provided we come with humble penitence and lively faith.

CHAPTER 3

PASTOR AND PEOPLE PREPARE

The Priest standing at the north side of the Table shall say the Lord's Prayer with the Collect following, the people kneeling. By custom the Lord's Prayer at the beginning of the Communion Service is said by the celebrant alone. The historical reason for this is that it originally formed a part of the Priest's private preparation, which was an important part of the pre-Reformation service. No doubt the Reformers wanted to encourage personal preparation *before* coming to the Lord's Table, and so they removed all introductory matter except the Lord's Prayer. Some suggest that, lacking any direction to the contrary, the people also should join in saying it, especially in view of the rubric in Morning Prayer which says that they shall repeat the Lord's Prayer with the Minister "both here, and wheresoever else it is used in Divine Service".

Be that as it may, the almost universal practice of leaving the first Lord's Prayer to be said by the celebrant only has important lessons to teach. Article XXVI assures us that the unworthiness of Ministers does not hinder the effect of the Sacraments. They are effectual because of Christ's institution and promise, even though they be ministered by evil men. Comforting as this may be, a congregation likes to know that the one who leads them in worship is a true man of God. He is approaching the Sacrament with the same longings for holiness as they are. His need of grace is every bit as great as theirs; perhaps greater, for he has the care of souls on his heart. As he says the Lord's Prayer by himself the whole congregation may be lifting him up to God in silent supplication. "Lord, answer the prayer of this thy servant, that he who ministers to us in holy things may himself be sanctified."

Though this may be the primary thought, we can also feel that the Lord's Prayer is being offered on behalf of us all. It stands at the head of the service because it is the model for all our worship. Here it is in the original form given by our Lord, without the doxology. It sets the standard for the penitence and prayer which will follow. When the Lord's Prayer comes again after the Communion it has the doxology added, for it introduces the thanksgiving part of the service.

Perhaps, as Cosslett Quin points out,[1] we keep silence here because we are not really able to pray these words at all. In the voice of the Minister we hear the voice of Christ. He is teaching us to pray. But before we can pray for ourselves we need to grasp afresh the truth of our redemption. It is only after we have received the sacred symbols that we join to say "Our Father".

THE MODEL PRAYER

The Lord's Prayer is far more than a form of words to be said: it is a model for all our praying. Its opening words insist that prayer depends on relationship. "Ask the *Father*" is at the heart of our Lord's teaching on the subject. Until we know that God is our Father, prayer means very little. Jesus came not simply to teach us about the Fatherhood of God, but that we might be "made God's children by adoption and grace" (Collect of Christmas Day). "To all who received him, who believed in his name, he gave power to become children of God" (John 1:12). Further, this relationship of child to Father is not something to be enjoyed in splendid isolation. To be a child of God is to be a brother of all his other children. "When ye pray, say *Our Father*" (Luke 11:2 A.V.). Both words are essential to true worship.

As the prayer goes on we learn that our first concern is to be with God and not with our own needs. *Thy Name, thy Kingdom, thy Will*, come before any petition for ourselves. The trouble with most of our lives is that they are self-centred.

[1] *At the Lord's Table* (Lutterworth Press). p. 42.

Worship is the God-given opportunity to forget ourselves. But into our very prayers comes a preoccupation with our own needs: *my* work, *my* witness, *my* temptations become all-absorbing. The Lord's Prayer rebukes this. Let God be first: the hallowing of his Name, the coming of his Kingdom, the doing of his Will.

Yet when our own needs are mentioned, the first petition is about our daily bread. It is possible to read into this a request for the living Bread which sustains the soul. But its plain and literal meaning is that we are asking for the supply of our everyday wants. We are dependent on God for everything, and he is concerned with physical as well as spiritual life. Was not the Word made flesh? The Incarnation puts beyond all doubt the fact that God is involved in all that affects our daily life. We need not hesitate to bring to him in prayer the details of our earthly existence. He hallows all, just as in this service he will hallow the bread and wine and use them for his own purposes. But because our response to his grace is so partial and imperfect, we pray too for forgiveness, leading and deliverance. In this first Lord's Prayer we get a glimpse of what our Christian life ought to be.

THE COLLECT FOR PURITY

There follows the Collect for Purity. Like so many of the Collects, it is a translation of an older Latin prayer which was used in the Sarum Missal. There it was a part of the Priest's Preparation. It must be regarded as a divine providence that the ancient prayers of the Church were translated by such a master of the English language as Archbishop Cranmer. In depth of spiritual meaning and in beauty of rhythmical speech this Collect could scarcely be bettered. Here is the congregation putting itself deliberately under the influence of the Holy Spirit in order that the worship may be worthy of Almighty God.

Such worship must above all things be sincere. We may deceive others, and even deceive ourselves. But God who is almighty is also omniscient. Nothing escapes his all-seeing eye. "Before him no creature is hidden, but all are open and laid bare to the eyes of him with whom we have to do" (Heb. 4:13). Ever since "the man and his wife hid themselves from the presence of the Lord God among the trees of the garden" (Gen. 3:8) man has tried to cover up the traces of his wrong doing. Yet as the Psalmist wrote: "If I say, 'Let only darkness cover me, and the light about me be night', even the darkness is not dark to thee, the night is bright as the day; for darkness is as light with thee" (Ps. 139:11, 12).

God requires truth in the inward parts. He is the one *unto whom all hearts be open, all desires known, and from whom no secrets are hid*. Those words contain a promise of hope as well as a warning. When Hagar called the name of the Lord who spoke to her, "Thou art a God of seeing" (Gen. 16:13), she was referring chiefly to his watchful eye upon her. The evening hymn says:

> Thy kind but searching glance can scan
> The very wounds that shame would hide.

We may hang on to that fact. The searching glance is also kind. He sees the struggle in the heart, the desire for better things, the secret longing after holiness. We have nothing to fear if we are open with God. "He who conceals his transgressions will not prosper, but he who confesses and forsakes them will obtain mercy" (Prov. 28:13). Then we must hold nothing back from God who sees and knows all.

We cannot begin to worship apart from the inspiration of the Holy Spirit. As our Lord once breathed on his disciples and said to them, "Receive the Holy Spirit," so we ask him to do it again. That first symbolic act took place before Pentecost. We who live after Pentecost are heirs of the gift of the Spirit. Our entry into the Christian Family is by Baptism with water and the Holy Ghost. When we come to be in Christ, we receive the Holy Spirit. There is a definiteness about this initial step. We "were sealed with the promised Holy Spirit" (Eph. 1:13). But we need a constant renewing of the life which God has implanted.

So we pray God to *cleanse the thoughts of our hearts by the inspiration of thy Holy Spirit.* Later in the service we shall see that cleansing is in the precious blood of Christ. There is no other fountain opened for sin and uncleanness. Here it is the Holy Spirit who is to do his sanctifying work. He is within us : let him now inspire us. Let him come as the wind and blow away all the mists of doubt, all the selfish thoughts and ambitions of our inmost being, every unclean imagining; yes, and our wayward, *wandering* thoughts. We cast ourselves on God the Holy Ghost.

> *O Wind of God, come bend us, break us,*
> *Till humbly we confess our need;*
> *Then in thy tenderness remake us;*
> *Revive, restore, for this we plead.*

Surely it is as the Holy Spirit deals with our pride, and brings us humbly to confess our need, that we shall come to love God perfectly, and magnify his holy Name worthily. Our love will never in this life be perfect in an absolute sense, for perfection belongs to God alone. But it may be perfect in the sense that it comes from an undivided heart. They love most who are aware of their own sinfulness and are conscious of the greatness of the forgiving love of God. We worthily magnify his holy name, not by pretending to any worthiness of our own, but by taking our place as the sinners that Jesus came to save. The worship which we owe to God can only truly flow from a heart which is lost in wonder, love and praise. It is the work of the Holy Spirit to bring us to the place where we forget ourselves, and are taken up with the completely surprising miracle of the grace of God.

CHAPTER 4

OUR SCHOOLMASTER

So far, in our approach to the Royal Banquet, we have stood afar off and asked for help from God that we may come in the right way. Part of the love and worship we are to offer is a humble confession of our need. Knowing how easily we can be complacent about our conduct if we have not some objective standard by which to measure it, the Reformers saw fit to introduce at this point the Ten Commandments. Doubtless they were influenced by Continental Reformers who had introduced the Commandments into their services. But a major reason for having them in the Ante-Communion was to ensure some degree of self-examination. Up to 1552 Auricular Confession had been widely used. Theoretically, at any rate, it had the effect of making people face up to their sins. When it was abolished as a regular practice, something had to be done to take the place of the Confessional.

The Ten Commandments certainly supply the need for self-examination. They are the basis of all morality, the laws which include all other laws. We must interpret them as our Lord did. He came, not to destroy the Law, but to fulfil it, i.e. to fill out its meaning. When we hear these words, and apply them to ourselves in the light of the New Testament, we find that we are among those who must needs, *after every Commandment, ask God mercy for their transgression thereof for the time past, and grace to keep the same for the time to come.* The Ten Commandments face us with an authoritative standard. We are left in no doubt about right and wrong because these are not the words of man. *God spake these words, and said—*

WORMSHIP

1. *I am the Lord thy God: Thou shalt have none other gods but me.* The Decalogue begins with an uncompromising statement that there is but one God, and he is the God whom Israel must worship. They were surrounded by heathen nations with their tribal deities, and there was a constant pull towards idolatry. It was fundamental to every part of their life that the Lord alone should be the object of their worship. It is fatally easy today to let something other than God take the first place. As Matthew Henry wrote in the seventeenth century: "Pride makes a god of self, covetousness makes a god of money, sensuality makes a god of the belly; whatever is esteemed and loved, feared or served, delighted in or depended on, more than God, that (whatever it is) we do in effect make a god of."[1]

2. *Thou shalt not make to thyself any graven image.* This is not just an expansion of the first Commandment. When the Israelites made an image, as in Exodus 32:4, they would have denied that they were worshipping a heathen deity. The image was merely a representation, to help them to worship the true God. But God forbids any such thing. Any image of God would certainly be inadequate, misleading and distorted. We who live in the Christian dispensation know that the perfect likeness of God once appeared on this earth. Jesus Christ "reflects the glory of God and bears the very stamp of his nature" (Heb. 1:3). Any view of God which sees him as different from the portrait of Jesus given in the Gospels is a graven image of our own imagination. The only way of ensuring that our worship of the one God shall be *in truth* (John 4:23) is constantly to check our conception of the Deity by reference to the Bible. The fact that so much of our Prayer Book worship is taken directly from the Bible is a safeguard against the breaking of this law.

God's jealousy is not to be confused with the horrid, yellow sin of human jealousy. He is a jealous God who cannot see the

[1] Matthew Henry's *Commentary* (Marshall Brothers) *in loc.*

glory given to another which by right belongs to him. That this uncompromising God should visit the sins of the fathers upon the children is a solemn reminder that sin bears fruit in succeeding generations. As physical weaknesses are sometimes passed on, so moral delinquency is likely to be reproduced in children and grandchildren. Thank God, the opposite is also true. The seed of the godly will also be godly. Those who love God and keep his commandments may look forward to many generations who will experience the mercy of the Lord. True godliness is vital, not only for our own sake, but for the sake of children yet unborn.

REVERENCE

3. *Thou shalt not take the Name of the Lord thy God in vain.* It is obvious that profane use of the Name of God is out of the question for a Christian. But there are other ways in which we take his Name in vain. This Commandment condemns all insincerity and hypocrisy. It is insincere to sing:

> *O for a thousand tongues to sing*
> *My great Redeemer's praise,*

if we have no intention of using the one tongue we have to confess Christ before men. What about the ease with which we can sing "Take my silver and my gold", while we put a quite inadequate coin in the collection? Our sincerity is not only tested by the words we say or sing in church. We need to watch the tendency to claim divine guidance for something which is really just what we want to do. "I did not feel led to do anything, or to say anything" may be no more than a rationalisation. If we were honest we should have to say, "I was too lazy to act, or too cowardly to speak."

Reverence is essential in all our worship and in all our life. We reveal a lack of it by unpunctuality in coming to services and by careless behaviour and slovenly posture in church. A text which might well be displayed in all our churches is: "The Lord is in his holy temple; let all the earth *keep silence*

C

before him" (Hab. 2 : 20). When we speak about God and our experience of him, there must be no light-hearted glibness, no second-hand retailing of a religion which is not quite our own, no talking for the sake of bringing glory to ourselves. The Pharisees who made long prayers at the street corners to be seen of men were certainly taking God's Name in vain. (See Matt. 6 : 5.)

THE LORD'S DAY

4. *Remember that thou keep holy the Sabbath Day.* One day in seven is set apart for rest and worship. With the Jews it was the seventh day, and there were strict laws about keeping it. The first Christians, who were all Jews, kept the Sabbath, but soon it became necessary to distinguish the two religions, and the Christians chose the first day. The Lord's Day thus became a weekly commemoration of the Resurrection. On it there was invariably the gathering of all believers for worship.

The Christian Sunday is to be a day of gladness. The cares of the week are to be set aside and full advantage taken of the opportunity for renewal of spirit, mind and body. This involves every Christian in the absolute obligation of Sunday worship. Only illness or other urgent cause may keep us from this. It also entails giving time on Sunday to prayer and reading, if only to let our souls catch up on what may have been poorly done during the week. For all who are not hindered by age or ill-health it should also give a welcome opportunity to engage in active Christian service. In addition to using our Sundays to the full, we should avoid anything which would unnecessarily deprive others of their day of rest, and use what influence we have to preserve the sacred character of the day.

The ultimate purpose of the Lord's Day is to ensure that all our time is dedicated to God and sanctified by him. Those who keep this Commandment will do so first and foremost because God has required it. But they will also find that, by making the Sabbath a delight, they are lightening the burden of the six days on which they labour and do all that they have to do.

HOME LIFE

5. Honour thy father and thy mother. In the Jewish community much importance was attached to family life, and this is enhanced in the New Testament. Part of the honour due to parents, St. Paul tells us, is obedience. "Children, obey your parents in the Lord, for this is right" (Eph. 6:1). The same passage speaks of the duties of parents, and of servants and masters. Home and family life are to be guarded as something sacred. Yet home is commonly the place where we behave worst, even though it is also the place where we are treated best.

If Christians do not maintain their family relationships in love and peace, what hope have they of living in the fellowship of the wider family of the Church? It is a matter of dispute whether the fifth Commandment belongs to the first or second table of the Decalogue: our duty towards God or our duty towards our neighbour. If the former is the case, it explains the divine institution of the family, parents being virtually in the place of God until children are old enough to know God consciously for themselves. If, as seems more probable, it is to be taken as part of our duty to our neighbour, it shows that our very first duty is towards our nearest neighbours, those in our own home. It is in the home that we appear as what we really are.

LOVE

6. Thou shalt do no murder. On the Christian application of this Commandment we are left in no doubt, for our Lord makes explicit reference to it. "You have heard that it was said to the men of old, 'You shall not kill; and whoever kills shall be liable to judgment.' But I say to you that every one who is angry with his brother shall be liable to judgment." (Matt. 5:21, 22). Jesus looks behind the action to the motive which prompts it. Men commit murder through anger, jealousy, hatred, malice and so forth. To have any of these things in our hearts is to break the Commandment in spirit. We must be reconciled to our brother before ever we can offer our worship to God.

The opposite of murder is not just to refrain from murder. The motive of that may be no more than to save one's skin. The true opposite of murder is love. Not to do good to people is really to do them harm. We have to consider how far the neglect of our opportunities has injured our fellow men. When our Lord asked the Pharisees if it was better on the Sabbath day to save life or to kill, he implied that if he had not healed the man he would have been committing murder. (See Mark 3:4.) St. John teaches that "any one who hates his brother is a murderer" and in the same paragraph says, "If any one has the world's goods and sees his brother in need, yet closes his heart against him, how does God's love abide in him?" (1 John 3:15, 17).

PURITY

7. *Thou shalt not commit adultery.* Again our Lord's interpretation is very clear. He enlarges the prohibition to include every kind of immorality, and makes it apply to thoughts as well as actions. There has been a wholesome reaction from the prudery of an earlier day when, with a complete disregard of theology, people thought there was something almost shameful about sex. Marriage has been more clearly expounded of recent years, and we speak openly of "the natural instincts and affections implanted by God". This is entirely in accord with Scripture, which emphasises that "marriage is honourable in all things" (Heb. 13:4. A.V.). All the more reason, therefore, why Christians should contend for a high standard of moral behaviour.

Marriage is sacred; sex is a gift of God. To defile the body by misuse of the sex instinct is sinful. It is in the context of his interpretation of this Commandment (Matt. 5:27-32) that Jesus spoke of plucking out the eye, and cutting off the hand, if they were a cause of offence. Such figurative language brings home the need to be ruthless in avoiding, wherever possible, anything that leads to temptation. The control of thoughts is the key to the situation, and in this the positive advice of St. Paul is: "Finally, brethren, whatsoever things are true, whatsoever things are honourable, whatsoever things are just, whatsoever things are pure, whatsoever things are lovely, whatsoever things are of good report; if there be any virtue, and if there be any praise, think on these things" (Phil. 4:8, A.V.).

HONESTY

8. *Thou shalt not steal.* There are more ways of breaking this Commandment than most people have ever thought of. An employer can steal by under-paying, a trader by over-charging, an employee by slacking. Honesty in every detail is what God requires, whether in income tax returns and customs declarations, or in much smaller matters. A Christian sees all his possessions as a trust from God, and the way in which money is spent is as important as the way in which it is acquired. "The love of money is the root of all evils" (1 Tim. 6:10).

In the Old Testament Law the tithe, or tenth part, of possessions was demanded as an offering to God. Though the behaviour of the Pharisees showed the danger of this degenerating into pure legalism (see Matt. 23:23), the giving back of one-tenth of income to God is to be recommended to Christians as normal. Since we are not under the law, but under grace, we are at liberty to adopt a different standard, but surely not a lower one. If a proportion of income is resolutely set aside for this purpose, it is found that greater care and responsibility is exercised in the use of what remains.

The contrast to stealing, as given by St. Paul, is interesting: "Let the thief no longer steal, but rather let him labour, doing honest work with his hands, so that he may be able to give to those in need" (Eph. 4:28). "Honest work" is the normal way of getting money. This is the law of labour. There is also the law of exchange, which covers all kinds of trading. And there is the law of love, which sanctions the right to receive a free gift, whether by inheritance or in any other way. Betting and gambling do not come within any of these laws, and it is difficult to see how a Christian can take part in them.

TRUTHFULNESS

9. *Thou shalt not bear false witness against thy neighbour.* Absolute truth is a far-reaching demand. A deliberate lie is easy enough to avoid, but there remains the misleading half-truth, the tendency to exaggerate, and even the silence which deceives. Christians need to cultivate an openness of character, and habits of conversation in which the yea is yea and the nay is nay. (See Matt. 5:37.) We need also to remember the injunction about "speaking the truth in love" (Eph. 4:15). Some people who boast of their plain speaking must watch whether their motive is *really* to edify, and not to hurt or wound.

False witness against our neighbours is inconsistent with that love which is the first of all the Commandments of the Law. Even if we know some scandal to be true there is nothing to be gained by passing it on. Gossip can be the ruin of a reputation, and it can also bring disaster to the one who gossips. It is salutary to remember that the faults we see and dislike most in others are those we refuse to face in ourselves. Conscience appears to be eased by finding someone whom we think worse than we are.

COVETOUSNESS

10. *Thou shalt not covet.* The final Commandment differs from all the others in that it prohibits, not simply an action, but a state of heart and mind. The New Testament is most emphatic about the sin of covetousness. "Take heed, and beware of all covetousness; for a man's life does not consist in the abundance of his possessions," said our Lord in introducing the parable of the rich farmer (Luke 12:15-21). Covetousness is idolatry (see Col. 3:5) for it sets the heart seeking *things* rather than God.

Positive obedience to this command implies contentment. "There is great gain in godliness with contentment; for we brought nothing into the world, and we cannot take anything out of the world; but if we have food and clothing, with these we shall be content" (1 Tim. 6:6-8). This does not mean that there is any virtue in poverty, or that all ambition is wrong. But discontent breeds unlawful desires for possessions, position or power, to serve one's own advantage. Little with God's blessing is better than much without it. "Keep your life free from love of money, and be content with what you have; for he has said, 'I will never fail you nor forsake you'" (Heb. 13:5). St. Paul had learned the secret of facing plenty and hunger, abundance and want, and he could say, "I have learned, in whatever state I am, to be content" (Phil. 4:11).

As we have seen, the chief purpose of having the Commandments read at this point in the service is to assist self-examination. "Through the Law comes knowledge of sin" (Rom. 3:20). The harder we try to keep the Law, the more conscious we are of our failure and inability. What St. Paul says of the Law historically is also true experimentally: "The Law was our schoolmaster to bring us unto Christ, that we might be justified by faith" (Gal. 3:24. A.V.). In Christ we find the mercy that forgives our transgression in time past, and the grace that empowers for the time to come. Hence the appropriateness of the petition: *Lord have mercy upon us, and incline our hearts to keep this law.* This amounts to a prayer that the absolute standards of God's perfect law may be our standards too. We dare not pray for anything less. "You, therefore, must be perfect, as your heavenly Father is perfect" (Matt. 5:48).

CHAPTER 5

THE COLLECTS

THE word "Collect" in the Prayer Book denotes a short prayer, and is not confined to the Collect of the particular Sunday or Holy Day. We have already noted the Collect for purity, and the term appears in Morning and Evening Prayer, the Order of Confirmation, the Visitation of the Sick and the Burial of the Dead. Its origin is variously explained, but there are only two suggestions to be seriously considered. One is that it was the prayer used when the people were assembled for worship, the word *collecta* referring to a collection of people, an assembly. The other is that it was the "collecting" of the petitions of the various members of the congregation into one concise prayer. Both explanations are of value. While it is undoubtedly true also that the Collect of the Day sometimes "collects" together the main thoughts of the service, that is not the original significance of the word. The derivation from *cum lectione*, "with the reading", is improbable.

FOR THE QUEEN

The two prayers for the Queen, which follow the Commandments, are called Collects, though they are not typical of the Collect as it has come down to us from the remote past. In the first and second English Prayer Books one of them was to be said *after* the Collects of the Day. This was reminiscent of the pre-Reformation service, where intercessions of various kinds were inserted in the same place. The change of position to *before* the Collect has the practical advantage of avoiding having to turn back from the Collect and back again to the Epistle. Actually, in 1662 there was a political motive in placing the prayer in this position, since, following the period of the Commonwealth, it was desired that clergymen should show their loyalty to the King right at the beginning of the service.

Some doubt the rightness of having these prayers in this particular place. They seem to interrupt the flow of the Ante-Communion which is so largely the ministry of the Word. But a good case can be made for retaining them. Prayer for rulers and all in authority was enjoined by St. Paul in 1 Tim. 2:1, 2, and he put them first on the list of people to be prayed for. In his day this meant praying for Nero. Our Christian life is not lived in a vacuum. Our citizenship is in heaven, but we belong also to an earthly state. We are to render to Caesar the things that are Caesar's. To be a good Christian is to be a good citizen.

The actual wording of the two prayers savours somewhat of the absolute monarchy of Tudor times. Both were written in 1549. Yet only a little imagination is required in the use of them to make them appropriate for today. The first seems to recognise that Church and Nation are one, a situation unhappily true only in theory now. That monarchs are God's chosen servants we surely still believe, and we enlarge our prayer by mentally including all who share the burden of government. To pray that we serve, honour, and humbly obey our Sovereign means more than personal loyalty to the Queen. We are to be responsible citizens. Wisdom says, in the Book of Proverbs, "By me kings reign, and rulers decree what is just" (8.15). The equivalent in the New Testament is: "There is no authority except from God, and those that exist have been instituted by God" (Rom. 13:1).

The alternative prayer contains the undoubted truth that the Bible teaches God's over-ruling providence. The prayer is that the Queen may, in all her thoughts, words, and works, seek God's honour and glory. As Her Majesty's Royal Assent is required to everything that Parliament enacts, this surely is a comprehensive prayer. If we remember that the original meaning of "wealth" is not merely monetary riches, but complete well-being in the highest sense, we see the appropriateness of a

prayer that all the people of the Commonwealth may be pre-
served in wealth, peace and godliness.

COLLECT OF THE DAY

We turn now to the Collect of the Day. In common speech
it is sometimes called the Collect *for* the Day, but this is in-
accurate. In Morning Prayer we have the Collect *for* Peace and
the Collect *for* Grace. It is better to adhere to the prepositions
used in the rubrics. The Collects are of two kinds: those taken
from ancient sources of the fifth and sixth centuries, and those
composed by the Reformers. The former were in the Sarum
Missal, and were translated from the Latin by Archbishop
Cranmer. From this source come all the Sunday Collects except
the first three in Advent, and Christmas I, Quinquagesima and
Epiphany VI. The Reformation Collects are mainly those of
the Saints' Days.[1]

There is a general plan of structure in a Collect, though it
is not invariably followed. It begins with the invocation of
God's name, together with the mention of one or more of his
attributes. A good example of this is Trinity VII, "Lord of all
power and might." Others are "Almighty and everlasting God"
(Trinity XII) and "Almighty and merciful God" (Trinity XIII).
Whitsunday has the single word "God". All, except the Collects
of Advent III, St. Stephen and Lent I, are addressed to God the
Father, while the three mentioned are addressed to our Lord.
It is the more normal practice in the New Testament to pray
to the Father, in the Name of the Lord Jesus. The prayer of St.
Stephen at his martyrdom, "Lord Jesus, receive my spirit,"
shows that there can be exceptions.

The invocation of God's name is followed as a rule by mention of some fact which is the basis of the petition. Thus in
the Collect of Trinity VII we have "who art the author and

[1] For details of the origin of each Collect, together with comments
and general information, reference should be made to the volume
in this series entitled *The Collects* by the Rev. L. E. H. Stephens-
Hodge.

giver of all good things". Each of the examples cited in the preceding paragraph follow this pattern. Trinity XII has "who art always more ready to hear than we to pray, and art wont to give more than either we desire or deserve", which is really two related facts. Trinity XIII gives us "of whose only gift it cometh that thy faithful people do unto thee true and laudable service". Whitsunday, with its abrupt address, "God," amplifies it with the words "who as at this time didst teach the hearts of thy faithful people, by the sending to them the light of thy Holy Spirit".

The next component part of the Collect is the petition itself. Sometimes there may be two or more connected petitions. Trinity VII again furnishes us with a good example: "Graft in our hearts the love of thy Name, increase in us true religion, nourish us with all goodness, and of thy great mercy keep us in the same." The Collect of Trinity XIX, in which the invocation and the ground of the plea are contained in the words, "O God, forasmuch as without thee we are not able to please thee," has as its petition: "Mercifully grant that thy Holy Spirit may in all things direct and rule our hearts."

In some instances, though by no means in all, there is a mention of the purpose for which the petition is offered, the result which will follow as an answer to the prayer. Thus the prayer for pardon and peace in the Collect of Trinity XXI is "that they may be cleansed from all their sins, and serve thee with a quiet mind". In Trinity VI we ask God to pour into our hearts such love toward him "that we, loving thee above all things, may obtain thy promises, which exceed all that we can desire". This part of a Collect is sometimes called the Aspiration.

The concluding words are usually a pleading of the name or the merits of Christ, sometimes with an ascription of praise to the Holy Trinity. Thus we are reminded that all prayer must be in the name of our blessed Lord. We have no right to enter the presence of God except through Jesus. And all our praying must be primarily for the glory of God and not for our own well-being. Much of our praying can be selfish, but the Collects keep us seeking first the Kingdom of God and his righteousness.

Cranmer's translations of the ancient Collects retain much of the terseness of the original Latin. Those who like long and wandering circumlocutions in public worship may find the Collects over-short, terse and pointed. This was an objection raised by the Puritans. But today many Free Churchmen are finding the value of the Collects. It is precisely their ability to say so much in a few words which appeals so strongly. For example, what a wealth of theology, and of ardent desire, is in the Collect of Sexagesima: "O Lord God, who seest that we put not our trust in anything that we do; Mercifully grant that by thy power we may be defended against all adversity; through Jesus Christ our Lord."

CHAPTER 6

THE MINISTRY OF THE WORD

WHEN, on Whitsunday 1549, the people went to church and used the Book of Common Prayer for the first time, they might have noticed a number of changes from the services formerly held. But the difference which overshadowed every other change was the use of the English language instead of Latin. It was the great desire of the Reformers that the people should hear the Word of God in their own tongue. Though this appeared to be an innovation, it was no more than a return to the practice of primitive times.

Christian worship owed much to the worship of the Jews, and the reading of the Scriptures was an important part of the synagogue service. Naturally at first the Old Testament would be read at the meetings of Christians, and gradually, as letters from St. Paul and others came into circulation among the Churches, they were given an equal place of honour. As a generation came who had never known one of the apostles, the written records of the life and words of Jesus became very important. So before very long there were readings from the Old Testament, the Epistles, and the Gospels. Second-century writers, like Justin Martyn and Tertullian, mention the reading of apostolic books at the Holy Communion. Long before the Reformation the reading of an Old Testament lesson before the Epistle had dropped out. The Prayer Book does in fact intro-duce an Old Testament reading, namely the Ten Command-ments, but this hardly takes the place of the older lesson. There is much to be said for a re-introduction of a reading from the Old Testament, as has been done in the liturgy of the Church of South India.

THE EPISTLE

The first reading is almost invariably from one of the Epistles so that it is not surprising that it is known as the Epistle, even in those exceptional instances where it is taken from another part of the Bible. The exceptions are more common on Saints' Days than on Sundays, and they consist of passages from the Old Testament, the Acts of the Apostles, and the Book of Revelation.

The Epistle usually brings us practical instructions for Christian living. Doctrine is seen to be relevant to behaviour. Modern translations of the Epistles have helped to make our generation see that they are live letters, written to real people in actual situations. Yet, because they deal with principles which are timeless, they speak to our needs today. We listen as those who wait for a word of command. No direction is given about sitting or kneeling. In most churches it seems to be the custom to sit, the normal attitude when listening. If kneeling is the posture adopted, it emphasises our readiness to submit to God's Word.

And the Epistle ended, he shall say, Here endeth the Epistle. So runs the rubric. No such direction is given about the Gospel, presumably as a witness to the fact that the Gospel of our Lord and Saviour is never-ending. A story is told (though it is probably apocryphal) of a young man who was chosen to read the Gospel at his Ordination. In his nervousness he forgot himself, and finished by saying, "Here endeth the Gospel." The Bishop was heard to mutter : "God forbid, brother !"

THE GOSPEL

For the Gospel we are directed to stand. While "all Scripture is inspired by God and profitable" (2 Tim. 3 : 16) the Gospels are a kind of Holy of Holies. Here we see Christ himself, and hear his very words. While we reverence and obey God's Word brought to us through the inspired writers, we show a special reverence to the Word made flesh. When, as during Holy

Week, the Gospels are somewhat long, all except the aged and infirm should count it a privilege to stand in honour of the passion of the Son of God. Incidentally, it is in the passion narratives, which occupy so large a place in the four Gospels, that we notice particularly how restrained the evangelists are in their work. The story is told with unadorned simplicity.

Just as *the Epistle* is the term used for a particular part of the Communion Service, so *the holy Gospel* refers to that part which consists of a reading from one of the Gospels. In the rubric the word "Gospel" is used in two different senses: first, to denote a portion of the liturgy, and secondly, in the sense of one of the four Gospels. When the Gospel is announced, it is customary in many churches for the congregation to say or sing *Glory be to thee, O Lord*. This was directed in the first English Prayer Book (1549), but the second (1552) omitted it. Possibly it was thought that even this degree of responding tended to break the continual course of the reading of the Scripture.[1] No direction is found in our present Prayer Book, but the Scottish liturgy re-introduced it, together with the response at the end of the Gospel, *Thanks be to thee, O Lord*. The Prayer Book as proposed in 1928 gave alternative wording for these responses.

This is not the place to go into a detailed analysis of the Epistles and Gospels. For expository thoughts on them, reference should be made to the two relevant volumes in this series of Prayer Book Commentaries. Suffice it to say that the choice of passages to be read is largely the same as was in the Sarum Missal. The Reformers never introduced changes simply for the sake of change. It is often easy to see the connection between the Epistle and Gospel, but not invariably so. Taken as a whole they supply us with the facts of the Gospel, and the doctrines and practical exhortations most needed in a full-orbed Christian life.

[1] See *Concerning the Service of the Church* at the beginning of the Prayer Book.

THE SERMON

After the Gospel, the Nicene Creed is said.[1] This is dealt with separately in the next chapter. Following the Creed, and before the Sermon, the notices are to be given out. The first, according to the rubric, are to be concerned with the holy days, or fasting days, which are to be kept during the week. Then notice is to be given of the Communion. The phrase in brackets (*if occasion be*) is hardly necessary today when a weekly celebration of Holy Communion is recognised as a bare minimum. Then follow Briefs, Citations and Excommunications. Briefs are letters authorising collections for some special object. Citations are summons to appear before an ecclesiastical court. Excommunications are public expulsions from participation in the Church's life. All three are rarely, if ever, heard today, since other methods have been found of dealing with such situations as may arise.

The rest of the rubric defines the limits of what may suitably be given out in church. Some even doubt the wisdom of interrupting the devotional progress of the service by making any announcements at all. But there is another way of looking at this. All the activities of a church and parish should be such as can be offered to God as part of the worship of his holy Name. Giving the notices at this point is a way of reminding the congregation of this.

Then shall follow the Sermon. This is the only place in the Prayer Book, apart from the Solemnization of Matrimony, where a sermon is enjoined. But the Act of Uniformity Amendment Act of 1872 regularised existing practice by permitting sermons to be preached at any service, or even, as in the case of university sermons, simply preceded by a Collect or the Bidding Prayer. It is strange that the Holy Communion is often now the one Service at which no sermon is given. The recovery of the Ministry of the Word at the Lord's Supper, now happily becoming common, is a welcome return to primitive use.

[1] or sung. See p. 53.

Let us be perfectly clear about this, that true preaching is a Ministry of the *Word*. The truth of God, from the Bible, passes through the personality of the preacher, and is mediated to the people. If the preacher dares to proclaim his own notions instead of God's Word, he is an unfaithful steward. Sermons that start from some topic of the day are seldom of much value. Those that begin with the Bible, and draw out from a passage, a verse, or even a phrase, what the Bible teaches, will always be found to be relevant. Familiar stories come to life, and speak to the contemporary situation.

It is important that this should happen *at the Communion*. There must be no divorce between Word and Sacrament. Both are vehicles of God's grace. The Word is a necessary safeguard against the possibility of a religion which is purely mechanical, or even magical. The Sacrament ensures that it shall be more than an intellectual assent to the Gospel.

Training in preaching is now an important part of the preparation for the Ministry. It was not always so. At the Reformation few of the clergy had the knowledge or the ability to preach, and the two books of Homilies were produced to supply the lack of sermons. The rubric suggests that more Homilies might follow, but this never happened. Those that we have would, for the most part, be too long for modern use, and the style is archaic. But they serve as a splendid reminder of the seriousness of the preacher's task, for they deal most precisely with the doctrines and duties of the Christian life. It would be well if all congregations were as diligently instructed and as faithfully exhorted as those would be whose spiritual diet was the books of Homilies.

To some extent a congregation gets the kind of sermon it deserves. Preaching is not the work of one man but of the whole people of God. The sermon is as much a communal act as is the receiving of the Sacrament. It behoves every Christian to pray, and to hear with faith, that the Word of God may have free course and be glorified.

D

CHAPTER 7

I BELIEVE

THERE are few things more moving than the sight of a congregation of devout worshippers saying the Creed. That the first word is "I" and not "We", emphasises that faith is an individual matter. Yet the fact of saying it together brings out the corporate aspect of our affirmation. It is wholly fitting that, as in Morning and Evening Prayer, so in the Holy Communion, the Creed should follow the reading of God's Word. Having listened to the Epistle and Gospel, we declare that these are the things we believe, it is this by which we live.

There are of course three Creeds which, as members of the universal Church, we accept. The earliest, and simplest, is the Apostles' Creed, so called because it contains a summary of the apostolic teaching, as found in the New Testament. It originated as a declaration of faith to which converts were required to assent before they were baptized.

Early in the fourth century the Church was beset with the problem of the Person of Christ: how was he both *God* and *Man*? There was a real danger (humanly speaking) that the heretical Arius might carry the day with his contention that Jesus was something less than God. He would admit only that he was "of *like* substance with the Father". Athanasius, the champion of orthodoxy, insisted that he was "of *one* substance with the Father". It is a difference of only one letter in the Greek, but Athanasius saw that the essential deity of Christ was at stake. As this special phrase was introduced at the Council of Nicea, the Creed which contains it is called the Nicene Creed.

The third Creed, "commonly called the Creed of St. Athanasius", originated in the sixth century in Gaul, and expresses the Church's belief about two great mysteries, the Holy Trinity and the Incarnation.

It is the Nicene Creed that we recite at the Holy Communion. Those who have professed their faith, at Baptism and Confirmation, in the words of the Apostles' Creed, should now be in a position to enter more deeply into the doctrine of Christ. They are therefore required to say this fuller Creed. In these days when pseudo-Christian bodies abound, denying the deity of Christ, it is well that all communicants should know and understand the true faith of the gospel.

GOD THE FATHER

I believe in one God the Father Almighty. There is no comma after the word *God*, and strictly speaking the clause should always be said as a whole. If a pause is made after *God*, it *can* give the impression that the one God we believe in is the Father, while in fact he is the Trinity in Unity. Belief in "God the Father, who made me and all the world" (Catechism) makes all the difference to life. If God is our Creator, we know that we are here for a purpose, a part of his creative plan. God's purpose for us can never be at the expense of his purpose for the rest of the world. The whole of life, and the whole of history, is a mosaic put together by a master hand. To see the truth of God as Creator is to renounce all thought of exploiting others for our own ends.

GOD THE SON

The second paragraph of the Nicene Creed, as of the Apostles' Creed, is a recitation of the saving acts of God in Christ. Here we learn to believe "in God the Son, who hath redeemed me, and all mankind" (Catechism). But since by the fourth century (for reasons already stated) it had become necessary to define closely the deity of the Son of God, much attention is given to this point. All that Christ did is of no avail if he is not truly God. The use of the word *begotten* is important. On the physical plane, what is begotten shares the very nature of the one who begets. So when Christ is said to be God's "only begotten Son" (John 3:16 A.V.) it implies that he shares the very nature of the Father. He is God (begotten) of God, Light (begotten) of Light, Very (or genuine) God (begotten) of Very (or genuine) God. In our English version it is necessary to make a very brief pause after the words *God, Light, Very God*. This will show the meaning of the original Greek, which is that the Son is *God, out of God*. Far from having been created, even before time began, he is himself the agent in creation, since *by* (or through) *him all things were made. Being of one substance with the Father*, the Son is *God* in the same sense as the Father is God.

Yet our salvation depends upon a Saviour who, as well as being as divine as the Father, is also as human as ourselves. The early Church had to condemn as heretics those who held faulty views of the true *humanity* of our Lord. *For us men and for our salvation* he *came down from heaven, and was incarnate*. Apart from this he could never have borne our sorrows and our sins. The great miracle is that the Son of God should have been made man. If we accept that, we need not be stumbled by the manner in which it happened: *by the Holy Ghost of the Virgin Mary*. The unique event of the Incarnation took place in a unique way.

Our Lord's perfect manhood means that once in the whole of history a human life has been lived in every detail as God intended we should live. We have all fallen infinitely short of the standard. Jesus Christ was the only one who, as both God and man, could deal with the sin of the world. This was what he came to do, and it involved him in the suffering and death of the Cross. By passing directly from the Incarnation to the Crucifixion, the Creed does not belittle the importance of our Lord's earthly life. It rather emphasises the centrality of the Cross. This ugly reality took place here on earth, at a given time in history when Pontius Pilate was governor of Judea.

The same Cross, which reveals man at his lowest, shows Christ at his highest. He died as the Lamb of God, bearing away the sin of the world. It was the victory of love. And because Christ was victorious on Calvary, it was impossible that death should hold him. *And the third day he rose again according to the Scriptures.* The New Testament is very clear that in his Death and Resurrection Christ was fulfilling the prophecies of the Old Testament. His Resurrection is the vindication of his claim to be the Son of God (Rom. 1:4), and the pledge of our glorification (1 Cor. 15:20). It was followed inevitably by his return to the Father's right hand, where he always lives to make intercession for us (Heb. 7:25).

Our Lord's Ascension was the occasion of a promise that he "will come in the same way as you saw him go into heaven" (Acts 1:11). Indeed the fact of the Second Advent is one of the dominant themes of the New Testament. Excessive dogmatism about the interpretation of prophecy has made some Christians tend to neglect the doctrine entirely. This is to miss the inspiration of what St. Paul calls "our blessed hope" (Titus 2:13). The Creed concentrates our thoughts on two great certainties of the Coming: it will be to judge all men, and to establish his Eternal Kingdom. Every time we come to the Lord's Table it is to proclaim the Lord's death *until his coming again.*

GOD THE HOLY SPIRIT

In the third paragraph we learn to believe in "God, the Holy Ghost, who sanctifieth me, and all the elect people of God" (Catechism). From beginning to end our spiritual experience is made possible by the Holy Spirit. And he works in us within the fellowship of God's people. It is a sad fact that many who have a reasonable understanding of God the Father, and God the Son, are at a loss when they think about God the Holy Ghost. The Nicene Creed has certain important emphases. First, he is *the Lord*. The word denotes that he is a divine Person, as much a Person and as much God as is our Lord. Secondly, he is the *giver of life*. For clarity it would be well if a comma were inserted after "Lord". He is the Lord in an absolute sense.

He is also the giver of life. The Spirit is the agent of new birth (John 3:5). That he proceeds from the Father *and the Son* is a statement which has caused controversy in the Church, but our Lord did say that he himself would send the Spirit from the Father (John 15:26). And no Christian would deny that the Holy Spirit is equally worshipped and glorified with the Father and the Son. He is also the inspirer of the Bible, *who spake by the prophets.*

THE CHURCH

When the Holy Spirit was given on the Day of Pentecost there was established the *one Catholick and Apostolick Church.* Hitherto God's dealings had been through his chosen people Israel. Now Christ had broken down the barriers and the Holy Spirit was to create a *universal* Church. It is *catholic* in the sense that it is one all over the world, and one all down the centuries. It is *apostolic* because it is "built upon the foundation of the apostles and prophets, Christ Jesus himself being the chief corner stone" (Eph. 2:20). It is ruled by the apostolic doctrine as it is given in the Scriptures. Though its *unity* is marred by outward divisions, there is in reality only one Church, and never can be more. The word *"holy"* is omitted in the English translation, but more recent scholarship has shown that it was there in the original Greek version. Holiness, along with unity, catholicity and apostolicity, is certainly one of the marks of the Church.

We note that the Creed does not state, "I believe *in* one Catholick and Apostolick Church." This form is reserved for the three Persons of the Trinity; for faith, in the sense of personal commitment, is in God alone. We believe in the fact of the Church and accept its witness to the Holy Scriptures as divine truth. Similarly *I acknowledge one Baptism for the remission of sins.* Baptism is initiation into Christ and his Church. This initiation is *with a view to* the remission of sins. There is only one way of salvation, through acceptance of the grace of Christ freely bestowed, without reliance on any supposed merit of our own. The administration of Baptism to infants, before ever they are capable of a response, helps to emphasise that it is all of grace. Faith leads to hope, so *I look for the Resurrection of the dead, and the life of the world to come.* Though both have a reference to the future, there is also a sense in which the Christian experiences them now. St. Paul says: "And you he made alive, when you were dead . . ." (Eph. 2:1). Nevertheless it is well to be reminded that it is not only in this life that we have hope in Christ. (See 1 Cor. 15:19.)

The Nicene Creed is more than a theological statement. It is a battle hymn, calculated to rouse the Christian soldier to strenuous warfare for Christ and his Church. The rubric orders that it shall be *sung or said.* Even if it is commonly said rather than sung, it should never degenerate into a merely personal act of piety. Here is the army of the Lord professing its allegiance to the King.

CHAPTER 8

THE OFFERTORY

Then shall the Priest return to the Lord's Table, and begin the Offertory, saying one or more of these Sentences following, as he thinketh most convenient in his discretion. A mistake which is commonly made is to use the word "offertory" as the equivalent of "collection". It should be used only to denote that part of the Communion Service which we are now considering, and which includes the reading of one or more sentences from Scripture, the receiving of money gifts and presenting and placing them on the Holy Table, and the placing thereon also of sufficient bread and wine for the number of communicants present.

In primitive times it was the custom for the people to bring the bread and wine for use at the service. Now the elements are provided, as a rubric at the end of the service directs, *by the Curate and the Churchwardens at the charges of the Parish.* The offering of the people is made in money rather than in kind, but the placing of bread and wine on the Table *at this point* seems to connect it with the devotions of the people. Just as the bread and wine are the raw materials which God is going to use in the Sacrament of the Body and Blood of Christ, so the money, symbolic of the bringing of our lives "just as they are", can be taken and used by God to bring glory to him.

THE PURPOSE OF THE OFFERTORY

It is ordered, also in a rubric at the end, that *the money given at the Offertory shall be disposed of to such pious and charitable uses, as the Minister and Churchwardens shall think fit.* Two points need to be noted here. Unlike collections at other services, which are at the disposal of the Parochial Church

Council, Offertory alms must be allocated by the Minister and Churchwardens. Secondly, this money cannot rightly be used for paying church expenses, but must be put to pious and charitable uses. There is no "charity" in paying for the upkeep of the church in which we ourselves worship. Moreover, since this direction is contained in the Book of Common Prayer, which is itself annexed to an Act of Parliament, it has the force of law.

Giving money in the collection is only a small part of the surrendering of the whole of our lives to the judgment and mercy of God. But because it is often the last part of a man to be brought into subjection to the Law of Christ, what he does with his money may be symptomatic of his whole attitude to God. There is no suggestion here that there is any merit in our gift. The most generous gift in the world could never buy God's favour. All that we give is tainted with evil. Indeed it is only much later in the service, after we have actually received the Communion, that we offer ourselves, renewed in Christ Jesus, for his service. Here we bring our lives, in all their unworthiness, for God to deal with.

The gift of money at the Offertory will be but a portion of that part of our possessions which we have decided to give back to God. All that we have, our time and talents as well as our money, is his. This is the only point at which we begin to understand the meaning of Christian stewardship. In recognition of God's ownership of all, we restore a set proportion to him for his work. The Old Testament tithe, or tenth, is taken by many as a guide to determining the right amount. Yet Law is not the final word. The motive is love, and the example is Christ's offering of himself for us. Furthermore, "God loves a *cheerful* giver" (2 Cor. 9:7).

THE OFFERTORY SENTENCES

The verses of Scripture appointed for the Offertory are interesting. In the main they are chosen to encourage the spirit of generosity. In most of the sentences a different motive for giving can be seen. The three from 1 Corinthians 9, and the first of the two from Galatians 6, have to do with the support of the Ministry, a point to which the Puritans, at the Savoy Conference in 1661, took exception. They also objected to the two from Tobit. Yet surely, as Article VI says, the Church reads the apocryphal books, for example of life and instruction of manners, even though it does not apply them to establish any doctrine. There seems to be a tendency to use only a few of the sentences provided, and a variation of the one or more chosen is to be desired.

The duty of making the collection while the sentences are being read is assigned to *the Deacons, Churchwardens or other fit person appointed for that purpose.* The original Deacons, whose appointment is described in Acts 6:1-6, dealt primarily with the temporal affairs of the Church. Nowadays, when a Deacon is virtually serving an apprenticeship before being admitted to full Orders, this work is left to Churchwardens and Sidesmen. They should be, like the seven of those early days, "men of good repute, full of the Spirit and of wisdom". *The decent bason to be provided by the Parish for that purpose* is the alms dish. Nowadays the collection is made in bags or plates, which are then placed on the alms dish. It is probably better to use bags than plates as it is then easier to obey the Lord's words, "When you give alms, do not let your left hand know what your right hand is doing" (Matt. 6:3).

THE PRESENTATION

Great emphasis is placed on the way in which the collection is brought up. Those appointed for that purpose shall *reverently bring it to the Priest, who shall humbly present and place it upon the Holy Table.* These are directions about the outward manner in which it is done. But outward acts are the expression of inward states. We are here taught the duty of reverence in all that concerns our worship, not least in the ordering of our temporal affairs, and humility in our approach to God.

And when there is a Communion . . . We have already seen that before the Reformation there had been infrequent Communion. While the Reformers wished to remedy this, they did not succeed in achieving it all at once. It frequently happened that Ante-Communion, which includes the only rubrical direction for the preaching of a sermon, followed Morning Prayer, but no Communion was held. At the present time Ante-Communion is practically never heard without the Communion following, except perhaps on Good Friday, when it is desired to hear the Epistle and Gospel, but not to celebrate the Lord's Supper. Some would argue that Good Friday is, of all days, a suitable occasion for the Sacrament of our redemption. Others again would like to see an extension of the use of Ante-Communion, for instance as the context of a sermon at a week-day service intended to be chiefly devoted to the Ministry of the Word.

The placing of bread and wine upon the Table, as we have seen, is all that remains of the ancient custom of the people providing the elements for the Communion. The rubric does not even say that the Priest shall "humbly present" and place upon the Table so much as he shall think sufficient. In spite of this, the thought of bringing the bread and wine for God to use need not be excluded. They are his gifts, but they are also the product of man's labour. In a sense, any farmer, miller, baker or shopkeeper might be helping to provide the bread for the Sacrament. If he knew that he were doing so, would it make him more careful of the quality of his work? Ideally the answer is No, for all work should be to the glory of God, and the distinction between sacred and secular ought not to exist.

THE BREAD AND WINE

That *wine* means the fermented juice of the grape is agreed by all except a few who would like to use unfermented grape juice. There is, however, considerable controversy over the type of bread to be used. A rubric at the end of the service reads: *And to take away all occasion of dissension, and super-*

stition, which any person hath or might have concerning the Bread and Wine, it shall suffice that the Bread be such as is usual to be eaten; but the best and purest Wheat Bread that conveniently may be gotten. Before the Reformation wafers were used, and in the 1549 Prayer Book they were continued, "but without all manner of print, and something more larger and thicker than it was". From 1552 onwards we have the direction that ordinary bread "shall suffice", and that became normal. Indeed Canon 20 of 1604 spoke of "fine white Bread".

Wafers are now commonly used in churches, but the loss in symbolism is great. In one respect only are they like the original bread used: they are unleavened. Our Lord took the bread which was on the table at the Passover Feast, the bread which his disciples were accustomed to eating. He broke it, and distributed to each a portion of the whole. St. Paul's language about all being partakers of the one loaf is meaningless if each communicant is given a complete wafer which was never part of a larger whole. It is on these grounds that the use of ordinary bread is to be preferred. Those who oppose the use of wafers on the ground that they are illegal, or that they necessarily imply erroneous doctrine, may find their case vulnerable. Bishop Gore, who was not biased in favour of what might by some be called "evangelical practice", suggested the abandonment of "the wholly unsymbolical practice of *separate* wafers in favour of the one bread, in some form leavened or unleavened". It would be unfair to quote Gore on this point without mentioning that in the same note he advocated the addition of water to the wine. Cosslett Quin sums up well when he says: "If wafers are materially convenient, bread is symbolically better."[1]

There is a natural tendency, and one with which we may have a good deal of sympathy, to dismiss details of ritual as wholly irrelevant. Nevertheless, as already noted, the outward accompaniments of worship express both devotion and doctrine. To ignore the meaning of symbols entirely is to belittle

---

[1] *At the Lord's Table* (Lutterworth Press) p. 102.

the whole principle of Sacraments. This truth can be held in combination with another, namely that over-emphasis on the minutiae of ritual tends to pharisaism. In the Offertory, as in every other part of the service, the state of the heart is what matters most.

CHAPTER 9

THE GREAT INTERCESSION

INTERCESSORY prayer has always been a part of Christian worship. Up to and including the Prayer Book of 1549, intercession was included in the very long Prayer of Consecration. By 1552 there was a strong reaction against the teaching that in the Eucharist there is a re-presentation of the sacrifice of Calvary, and therefore that God is more ready to hear prayer at that time than at any other. Accordingly the makers of the second Prayer Book removed the intercessory part of the prayer to its present position, where it is the climax of the Ante-Communion. Another change made in 1552 was the addition of the words *militant here in earth* in the bidding. Previously it had read: "Let us pray for the whole state of Christ's Church." Prayer for that part of the Church which has already passed on was deliberately omitted by the Reformers.

The Prayer for the Church Militant begins with a clear reference to St. Paul's words in 1 Timothy 2:1-2: "First of all, then, I urge that supplications, prayers, intercessions, and thanksgivings be made for all men, for kings and all who are in high positions, that we may lead a quiet and peaceable life, godly and respectful in every way." The prayer itself reflects even the language of this passage, e.g. *that under her we may be godly and quietly governed*. It is important to note the breadth of the apostolic injunction—*for all men*. And we are not to omit the giving of thanks. Much of our praying tends to be too limited in its scope.

The first petition is connected with the Offertory, asking God to accept our alms and oblations. Some interpret the two words as referring to gifts for the poor and gifts for other objects respectively. Others see a reference to the gifts of money and the placing of bread and wine on the Holy Table. It is not a point worth arguing about, though a good deal has been written on both sides. We also ask God to *receive these our prayers*. Such a petition has added meaning if special subjects for prayer have been mentioned at the beginning, a custom now commonly adopted.

THE CATHOLIC CHURCH

Special prayers, however, whether for matters in the parish or beyond it, must not blind us to the needs of the *universal* Church. The story is told of a Vicar who was so impressed by the preacher from the Melanesian Mission that he said: "Let us pray for the whole state of Christ's Church militant here in earth—and in Melanesia!" Our prayer is each time for the *whole* Church, though it may be sometimes *specially* for a particular part. So we ask for the continual inspiration (by the Holy Spirit) of *the universal Church with the spirit of truth, unity and concord*. How much richer is our conception of the universal Church today than was possible to the compilers of the Prayer Book four hundred years ago. Not only is the Church planted in every land, but by the instantaneous transmission of news we become aware of needs here and there throughout the world which can be brought into our prayers and supplications for all men.

Truth, unity, and concord are essential to the life of the Church. All who profess and call themselves Christians, as the Prayer for All Sorts and Conditions of Men puts it, are not necessarily in the way of truth. So we pray here *that all they that do confess thy holy Name may agree in the truth of thy holy Word*. The Church's doctrine is based on Holy Scripture. Unity is one of the marks of the Church, but as it is sadly lacking it needs to be the subject of continual and fervent prayer. Unity need not mean uniformity. There is room for variety of expression in the one Church, holding "the faith once delivered to the saints". Hence the need for "concord", which is the outworking of "godly love".

THOSE IN AUTHORITY

There follows the petition for all Christian rulers. We may ask why we should limit our prayers to those who are Christians, since St. Paul certainly did not. Again we may wonder whether *Kings, Princes and Governors* is the best description of the Heads of States in the world today. This is but one indication of the need for a wise revision of our Prayer Book. Yet whatever may be true of other nations, we rejoice that in the Church of England we pray for *thy servant Elizabeth our Queen; that under her we may be godly and quietly governed.* Our history is such that Church and State are intimately associated. The Sovereign is crowned in Westminster Abbey by the Archbishop of Canterbury. Our conception of monarchy has greatly changed since Tudor times, but never has the example and influence of the Royal Family counted for more.

The request for those in authority under the Queen is that *they may truly and indifferently minister justice.* Misunderstanding of the word "indifferently" has caused many to substitute the word "impartially". Actually such a private amendment is not an improvement. We want those who administer our laws to be more than impartial. Their duty is to judge *what* is right rather than *who* is right. They are to stand by the truth with complete indifference to any consequences that may ensue. And while the law speaks in terms of punishing crime, and maintaining order, the Christian prays that this may result in *the punishment of wickedness and vice, and the maintenance of thy true religion, and virtue.* Obviously this involves us in prayer for those who *make* our laws, as well as those who enforce them. Not that people can be made virtuous by law, but in a country where the influence of Christianity has been so long predominant we should expect our laws to be such as uphold Christian standards.

THE MINISTRY

It is however the Church which, as the conscience of the nation, chiefly maintains true religion, and virtue. So we pray for grace to be given to *all Bishops and Curates*. As already noted, curates are those who have the cure of souls, the parochial clergy. As we now generally use the term to denote the *assistant* clergy, it would be better to pray, as in the Litany, for all Bishops, Priests and Deacons. The pastors of the flock are to be examples and teachers, setting forth God's true and lively Word *both by their life and doctrine*. Neither can have a real effect without the other, but holy living and clear teaching are a formidable combination. We notice too that the Word to be taught is not only true but *lively*. Some would have us substitute the word "living". While no doubt that is what "lively" meant in the sixteenth century, it is a pity to lose a picturesque and descriptive expression. An invalid can be said to be living, but only someone bursting with health and spirits is lively. Is it not true, as the Psalmist said, "His Word runs swiftly" (Ps. 147:15)?

Coupled with the setting forth of God's Word is the right and due administration of his holy Sacraments. In the Church of England there is a wholesome balance between the two. Article XIX states: "The visible Church of Christ is a congregation of faithful men, in the which the pure Word of God is preached, and the Sacraments be duly ministered according to Christ's ordinance in all those things that of necessity are requisite to the same." On the subject of the Sacraments, Article XXV says that there are two that are "ordained of Christ our Lord in the Gospel, that is to say, Baptism, and the Supper of the Lord". The Catechism, in answer to the question, "How many Sacraments hath Christ ordained in his Church?" replies: "Two only, as generally necessary to salvation, that is to say, Baptism, and the Supper of the Lord." The Reformers made it clear that these two are of the greatest importance. The whole of this book is designed to show the

E

nature of the Supper of the Lord. It should be remembered that Holy Baptism, the Sacrament of initiation into Christ and his Church, is equally vital. Its right and due administration is the constant care of the faithful pastor, and our prayer to this end is both necessary and appropriate. Moreover we need to be reminded that the laity are involved both in the setting forth of God's Word and in the administration of Baptism and Holy Communion.

THE PEOPLE OF GOD

The Church is not the clergy. When someone speaks of a young man "going into the Church" we know that he really means "going into the Ministry". We enter the Church at our Baptism. So we pray that to all God's people may be given grace. And because our prayers should be particular as well as general, we ask *specially for this congregation here present*. The burden of the prayer is that they may hear and receive God's holy Word, with meek heart and due reverence. We note with interest that here no reference is made to receiving the Sacraments. Can it be that this is included in hearing and receiving God's holy Word? This prayer is sometimes used when there is no Communion following. Then it asks quite simply that the Word read and preached may find an entrance into every heart. When there is Communion can it not also refer to the Word proclaimed in the breaking of bread? The effect of receiving the Word is service to God in holiness and righteousness continually. We are reminded of our Lord's prayer: "Sanctify them in the truth; thy word is truth" (John 17:17).

In holiness and righteousness all the days of their life is taken directly from the Benedictus (Luke 1:75). Perhaps "holiness" in this context refers to inward purity, while "righteousness" denotes outward acts of goodness. Both are to continue, and indeed to grow, "all the days of our life". But life is short. We are not in this world for ever, but only passing through, "in transit". It is in fact a *transitory* life. This is as true for the

holy and righteous as it is for the ungodly and wicked. Saint-
liness is no guarantee against *trouble, sorrow, need, sickness, or
any other adversity*. Our Lord's prayer is: "I do not pray that
thou shouldst take them out of the world, but that thou
shouldst keep them from the evil one" (John 17:15). Our prayer
for those in various kinds of trouble is that God will comfort
and succour them. While there will almost invariably be some
in the congregation itself who are in some kind of adversity,
our prayers should include a wider range. It is a real help if
special requests are mentioned as biddings at the beginning.

Whether life is long or short, mainly prosperous or full of
trials, it has one inevitable end. "It is appointed unto men once
to die, but after this the judgment" (Heb. 9:27, A.V.). For
those who are in Christ Jesus there is the assurance that there
is no condemnation (Rom. 8:1). They are "with Christ, which
is far better" (Phil. 1:23, A.V.). The Prayer Book therefore is
content to bless God's holy Name for them, and to pray that
we may be given *grace so to follow their good examples, that
with them we may be partakers of his heavenly kindom*. Thus
we retain our belief in the Communion of Saints, but carefully
safeguard it from the kind of abuses which had arisen before
the Reformation.

All prayer is offered through Christ. It is in his Name and
for his sake that we are heard. He is the one Mediator between
God and men (1 Tim. 2:5). And because he is truly man as well
as truly God, he pleads our cause as our Advocate. There can
never be any other Mediator or Advocate. Neither do we need
any other.

CHAPTER 10

THE EXHORTATIONS

PARTLY because of the modern passion for brevity, but also because Holy Communion is celebrated more frequently than was the case in the sixteenth century, the three long Exhortations are not often now heard. This is all the more reason for their being studied, for they contain sound doctrine related to practical living. The first two are alternatives, to be used when giving notice of a forthcoming Celebration of the Holy Communion; the third is intended to form part of the actual service. We shall look at each in turn.

THE FIRST EXHORTATION

1. All that a Minister does is *through God's assistance*. To those who are prepared to come he will administer *the most comfortable Sacrament of the Body and Blood of Christ*. This is an excellent definition of the Lord's Supper. We are concerned, not with the outward sign of bread and wine, but with the thing signified, "the Body and Blood of Christ, which are verily and indeed taken and received by the faithful in the Lord's Supper" (Catechism). This Sacrament is *to be by them received*. The climax of the service is the *receiving* of the consecrated bread and wine. For this reason the Prayer Book does not envisage attendance at the service without partaking. It was when our Lord gave to the disciples the bread and the cup that he said: "Take, eat; this is my body . . . Drink of it, all of you; for this is my blood." In the receiving we remember *his meritorious Cross and Passion*. Only through his atoning sacrifice do we *obtain remission of our sins, and are made partakers of the kingdom of heaven*.

If the Cross has obtained so much for us, we must needs be

thankful to God for his great gift of the Saviour, who both died for us, and is our spiritual food in the Lord's Supper. But the very dignity of the Sacrament places upon us a great responsibility to be properly prepared. For while it is *divine and comfortable* to those who receive worthily, it is *dangerous* to those who *presume to receive it unworthily*. As we have noted before, this is not a question of being worthy, in ourselves, to come. None of us is that. But we must be in earnest about our preparation. This includes heart-searching repentance and complete trust in Christ, so that we come to the Feast in the wedding-garment (Matt. 22:11). The man in the parable thought that he was good enough in his own clothes, and he passed muster until "the king came in to look at the guests".

How are we to prepare ourselves? The second paragraph of this Exhortation suggests four steps to be taken. First, examine yourself by the rule of God's Commandments. Again and again we come back to the Ten Commandments as the straight edge against which to measure the crookedness of our lives. A thorough examination on the lines suggested in Chapter 4 will reveal that we have offended *by will, word or deed*. Secondly, confess your sins to God. If this confession is sincere it will include *full purpose of amendment of life*. It is the sinner who confesses *and forsakes* his sins who obtains mercy (Prov. 28:13). And let this confession be definite. Without care in the stage of self-examination, it can too easily be vague. Thirdly, make restitution to any that you have wronged. This could mean not only restoring stolen property as Zaccheus did (Luke 19:8), but perhaps writing a letter of apology to one we have injured. Fourthly, be ready to forgive anyone who has sinned against you. If we do not repent in this genuine way, the Prayer Book says *the receiving of the Holy Communion doth nothing else but increase your damnation*. This latter word is taken from the Authorised Version of 1 Corinthians 11:29. A more correct translation is "judgment".

In view of the serious warnings in the Bible, the Church is undoubtedly right to exhort to repentance in this solemn way.

God is not mocked. Whatever the sin may be—and a few are mentioned by way of example—the alternative is plain: *repent you of your sins, or else come not to that holy Table.* Judas is taken as representing one who receives the Sacrament in a state of hardness of heart. Though it is by no means certain that Judas was present at the Lord's Supper itself, he was certainly there for most of the Passover meal which preceded it.

Because it is so essential that every communicant should come fully trusting in God's mercy, provision is made for those who cannot quieten their own conscience. Until 1552 Auricular Confession had been regularly used as an essential preparation for Communion. With the fuller understanding of the Gospel which was coming, people were now encouraged to accept God's pardon in Christ by simple faith. But it was recognised that some might need the help of a Minister of God's Word. Hence the invitation here given. It need not be regarded as normal: it is only *if there be any of you who by this means cannot quiet his own conscience herein.* Of this personal ministry of the clergyman to the troubled conscience we may say that it is there for all who need it, but it is not forced on any. Our Anglican practice in the matter may be summed up in the words: "None must; all may; some should." The last point would certainly be emphasised by many psychologists.

The phrasing of this invitation is to be noted as it gives a very different picture from the kind of sacramental confession practised before the Reformation. The seeker is to *come to me, or to some other discreet and learned Minister of God's Word.* The emphasis is upon the clergyman being a man of discernment (discreet) and well taught in the Scriptures. In other words, experience and knowledge are necessary, not merely the fact of being a Priest. Then, the penitent is to *open his grief,* and the healing benefit of absolution is to come *by the ministry of God's holy Word.* This is to be followed by spiritual counsel and advice. While some may prefer to seek such an interview in the more formal atmosphere of the church, where the relationship between counsellor and counselled is impersonal, others will find the informality of a quiet talk in the study of greater help, followed as it will be by prayer. Whatever the method, three things must be borne in mind. First, the seeker must be completely frank and open or he will be wasting time and harming his own soul. Secondly, it must be clearly understood that the Minister will never reveal to others what is confided to him. Thirdly there should be no hesitation in seeking spiritual help in this way. There are thousands of people who need this very thing in order that their spiritual experience may become clear, definite and happy.

THE SECOND EXHORTATION

2. The second Exhortation is to be used by the Minister *in case he shall see the people negligent to come to the Holy Communion*. It is largely based on the parable of the Great Supper in Luke 14:16-24. How can anyone refuse to come to the Feast, *being so lovingly called and bidden by God himself*? What would any man think if his friends treated him as we treat God by staying away? It is true that the parable refers to the acceptance or refusal of the Gospel itself, but its application to the Lord's Supper is surely permissible.

What are the excuses that people offer? One is *because I am otherwise hindered with worldly business*. This has a modern ring about it. In our material age many are busy all the week making money, and when Sunday comes are either too tired for spiritual exercise or too busy in house and garden to make time for worship. And all for what? *Such excuses are not so easily accepted and allowed before God*. Another excuse is *I am a grievous sinner, and therefore am afraid to come*. This of course is a reason not for staying away but for repentance while there is yet time. None of the excuses offered in the parable were accepted. Neither will ours be. So the Minister calls the people in a most moving exhortation, for Christ's sake and for their own sake, to come. For Christ's sake, because of his sacrifice for our salvation. For our sake, because we cannot escape if we neglect such a great salvation (Heb. 2:3).

One other aspect of the matter is worth noting. When we wilfully abstain from the Lord's Table, we *separate from our brethren who come to feed on the banquet of that most heavenly food*. So to stay away from the Holy Communion is to rob the Church of the fulness of its fellowship. It is an act of separation, a schism in the Body of Christ. The consideration of such things should certainly bring people to a better mind; and the earnest prayers of the pastor are directed to this end.

THE THIRD EXHORTATION

3. The third Exhortation is to be used at the time of the Celebration of the Communion. It begins with St. Paul's message about the duty of self-examination, and this for a two-fold reason : the great benefits derived from a true receiving of the Sacrament, and the great danger from an unworthy receiving. If we come aright *we spiritually eat the flesh of Christ, and drink his blood; then we dwell in Christ and Christ in us; we are one with Christ, and Christ with us*. These are very deep truths, and they are not dependent on our emotional reaction, but on facts appropriated by faith. If, on the other hand, we come unworthily, we eat and drink judgment to ourselves.

In the passage from which these words are taken, 1 Corinthians 11:29-30, St. Paul states that weakness and illness, and even death, had resulted from disorders at the Lord's Table. W. C. G. Proctor says of verse 30 : "It may be interpreted metaphorically as a description of their spiritual ineffectiveness; or it may be linked with the judgment of verse 29 and interpreted as a description of the physical evils which result from their excesses and which are the outward signs of God's condemnation."[1] The Prayer Book seems to take the latter view and connects it with the wrath of God. The expression is one which we cannot avoid if we take the New Testament seriously (John 3:36; Rom. 1:18). It signifies God's uncompromising opposition to all that is contrary to his will. Knowing what we do

[1] *New Bible Commentary* (I.V.F.) p. 984.

of the inter-action of body and spirit we cannot altogether deny that physical ills may result from a wrong relationship to God. So understood, the language of the Exhortation we are considering need not cause offence.

It is a very serious thing to be guilty of the Body and Blood of Christ our Saviour. We are so guilty when we do not *discern* the Lord's Body. This refers both to blindness as to the spiritual meaning of the Sacrament, and also failure to recognise the fact of the Church, the Body of Christ. It is sin against God and against our brother. If we would escape God's judgment, we must judge ourselves. The issue is very clearly put: turn from sin, trust in Christ, and show the reality of this faith by leading a new life of holiness and brotherly love. So *shall ye be meet partakers of these holy mysteries*. In this context the word "mysteries" is virtually "sacrament" or "symbols".

Self-examination, repentance and faith are only a part of the needful preparation. As we come to the Eucharist, the spirit must be filled with thanksgiving. In the subject for thanksgiving here set forth we have a quite priceless epitome of the Gospel. The object of our praise is God the Three in One, each of the Persons being involved in our salvation. Redemption was wrought by the Cross of Christ, and this he could accomplish because he is both God and man. In his humiliation he came to our level, and having been made sin for us bore the whole burden in himself. Thus we, *who lay in darkness and the shadow of death*, are made *children of God*, and exalted to *everlasting life*. How can we be kept in continual remembrance of so great a love and of such great benefits? The answer is: through the Sacrament which he instituted for this very purpose.

The outcome of thanksgiving is to be very practical: as the General Thanksgiving puts it, "not only with our lips but in our lives". The *continual thanks* which it is our bounden duty to offer must be accompanied by surrender and service. Submission to God's *holy will and pleasure* is a lifelong process of obedience. It means the acceptance of God's claims upon life in matters great and small. The first ambition of the Christian should be to please his Master, "to satisfy the one who enlisted him" (2 Tim. 2:4). This includes *studying*, i.e. giving dilligence, *to serve him in true holiness and righteousness*. Every Communion approached in the right way should find us a step further on in the path of obedience, and a more effective servant of the Lord who has done all for us.

CHAPTER II

THE INVITATION

THE preceding Exhortation has made clear what is required of those who come to the Lord's Table. In spite of an intense feeling of unworthiness— or perhaps even because of it—we still want to come. We know ourselves to be worth nothing, but are deeply grateful that we have a Saviour who bids us come. Here in this Invitation we are challenged to act upon what we know to be true.

We find ourselves among those who are addressed. *Ye that do truly and earnestly repent you of your sins.* Earnestness alone is not enough; there must be *true* repentance. Religious earnestness may be no more than grief because we have been found out and lost face before other people. True repentance is not just being sorry, but being so sorry that we want to forsake the sin. But a recognition of what we are will save us from formality and impart earnestness to our resolve.

Love and charity with our neighbours is one of the essentials which has been stressed in the opening rubric and in the first of the three Exhortations. We cannot be right with God if we are not right with our fellow men. No matter where the fault may lie, we are to do what we can for reconciliation. "If possible, so far as it depends upon you, live peaceably with all" (Rom. 12:18). We need to remember also that we can scarcely be said to be in love and charity with our neighbours if we are doing nothing at all to try and win them for Christ. Love wants to share.

As new possibilities of life in Christ open up before us we shall see how constantly we need to bend our intentions towards leading a new life. Each Communion beckons us on to greater heights. Even if there had been no slipping back, we should at least need to confess that our progress had not been more rapid. In actual fact, the nearer we come to God, the more conscious we are of our failure to follow his commandments and walk in his holy ways.

In this state of heart we are to draw near with faith. The two words *with faith* were added in the latest revision of the Prayer Book (1662). It seems that the custom had arisen of taking the words *Draw near* quite literally. At that moment in the service the communicants had left their places in the body of the church and come forward into the chancel. Helpful as that symbolism might be, it is good to emphasise that, even where such a practice would not be physically possible (as when there are too many communicants to find places in the chancel—happily a frequent occurrence) we can still draw near *with faith*. Let us not be lulled by the familiarity of the words into taking them as a matter of course. The whole miracle of divine grace lies in those words *Draw near*. Faith accepts the invitation, believing that God really means what he says.

Draw near . . . and take. There must be a receiving. Queen Esther not only approached the royal presence, she also put out her hand and touched the top of the sceptre (Esther 5 : 2). This was an act of faith in the honour of the King who had indicated his favour towards her. Too often we come rather hesitantly to God, and do not exercise the faith which takes him at his word. The Sacrament of the Lord's Supper teaches us otherwise. We receive. There is something very definite about it. There can be no doubt whether we have received or not. When we thus take *this holy Sacrament* it is to our *comfort*. Not that "comfort" is to be understood exclusively in its modern sense of "consolation". In its original meaning it has more to do with strengthening. We do not come to the Lord's Table to be given the kind of comfort which is associated with an armchair or a hot water bottle, but to obtain strength to go forth as a soldier to the fight.

In preparation we are to make our *humble confession to*

Almighty God. How confession could be anything but humble
it is difficult to see. Yet such is the subtlety of our fallen
nature that we can even be pleased with our own sincerity and
proud of our humility! In the first English Prayer Book the
Confession was to be to "Almighty God, and to his holy Church
here gathered together in his name". In 1552 it was altered to
"before the congregation". Whether the words are said or not,
it *is* a *public* confession of sin. We cannot confess to God what
we really are, and pretend to other people that we are something different. There could be only one attitude proper to the
Confession, and that is *meekly kneeling upon your knees*. The
punctuation makes it plain that"meekly" refers to the kneeling.
But inasmuch as posture is an outward mark of an inward
state, it is to be hoped that what follows will also be said in a
spirit of meekness.

CHAPTER 12

THE CONFESSION AND ABSOLUTION

Then shall this general Confession be made. There cannot be a *particular* confession of sins made by all the people, for the sins of one are not those of another. But a general confession includes us all, and the language of what follows is such that no one who is not incorrigibly self-righteous could fail to use it with meaning. It is directed to be said by one of the Ministers in the name of all the communicants. It is now invariably said by all, which is a far happier arrangement. The Confession was a new production at the Reformation, and owes much to the *Consultation* by Archbishop Hermann of Cologne, who was influenced by Martin Luther. There was no General Confession in the Sarum Missal, but only the Confession for the Clergy at the beginning of the Mass. As this included confession to "blessed Mary, all the saints and you" (the celebrant) it found no place in the Prayer Book.

THE CONFESSION

The Confession is addressed to *Almighty God, Father of our Lord Jesus Christ, Maker of all things, Judge of all men.* Language like that keeps us in our proper place. God the Almighty is our Creator and our Judge. Jesus Christ has revealed him as both these things. Yet when we consider Jesus Christ we think chiefly of him as Saviour, and rightly so. "Christ Jesus came into the world to save sinners" (1 Tim. 1 : 15). So when we address the Father of our Lord Jesus Christ we are speaking to the one whose chief concern is for our salvation. What depth of insight there is in the Collect of Trinity XI which says that God declares his almighty power most chiefly in showing mercy and pity. We confess to God who is before all else a *saving God.*

This does not make sin appear any less sinful. The more we know of the character of God the more are we conscious of *our manifold sins and wickedness*, and not only *acknowledge*, but *bewail* them. They are not vague, but definite things that we have done *from time to time*. In other words we are confessing more than a condition of sinfulness. Some of these sins have been committed by *thought*, some by *word*, some by *deed*. All have been done *most grievously*. If they have not grieved us as they should, they have certainly grieved God. They have affronted him who is both God and King—his *Divine Majesty*. How can he show anything but displeasure at our misdeeds? If we experience his wrath and indignation it is because we have provoked him. The language, as in the Old Testament, is anthropomorphic. We acknowledge that when God deals with our sins he is acting with perfect justice.

What can we do? *We do earnestly repent.* The sorrow which accompanies repentance is from the heart. This is the meaning of *heartily*, which has nothing to do with what in contemporary language we call heartiness. Godly sorrow for sin goes too deep for any display of levity or glibness. The remembrance of our sins is grievous to us because, as we have seen, they are grievous to God. *The burden of them is intolerable.* Is it? To many people those words seem to be an exaggeration, for they do not feel their sins as an intolerable burden. But here we must again point out that feelings are less important than facts. *Intolerable* means "unbearable". If we have to bear our sins upon ourselves, assuredly they are a burden too heavy to be borne. They will carry us down to destruction. If we want to know the weight of the burden we must consider what happened to him who "himself bore our sins in his body on the tree" (1 Pet. 2:24). Where should we be if we had to bear our own sins? The burden *is* intolerable. It behoves us to be intolerant towards our sins.

The cry is for mercy. "God, be merciful to me a sinner" (Luke 18:13). The tax collector who prayed that prayer went down to his house justified rather than the Pharisee who was full of his own goodness. The cry goes up to the *most merciful Father*. Moreover it is in the Name of the one who prayed on the Cross, "Father, forgive them; for they know not what they do" (Luke 23:24). In him there is a full and free forgiveness for *all that is past*. For this we ask. And because forgiveness is the establishment of a new relationship, we pray that we may go on to *serve and please* God *in newness of life*. As God answers our prayer of confession with his forgiveness, all the honour and glory must be given to him.

> *Who is a pardoning God like Thee,*
> *And who has grace so rich and free?*

THE ABSOLUTION

So important is it that we should know the certainty of God's pardon that it is declared to us in the form of the Absolution. The rubric tells us that if a Bishop is present, even if he is not the celebrant, he shall pronounce these words. They are to come to us with all the authority that attaches to the highest order in the Church. In the absence of the Bishop, the Priest who is taking the service will pronounce the Absolution.

In the services of Morning and Evening Prayer the Absolution is declaratory: "He pardoneth and absolveth all them that truly repent and unfeignedly believe his holy Gospel." Here it is imprecatory: *Almighty God, have mercy upon you*. There is a difference between a declaration, which would be "Almighty God . . . *has* mercy upon you", a prayer, which would be "(O) Almighty God . . . have mercy upon *us*"; and an imprecation, which is "*(May)* Almighty God . . . have mercy upon you". This form is very personal and direct.

First we are reminded that the God who grants his mercy is the God who has promised forgiveness to all who turn to him in repentance and faith. If we want a particular text to support this statement, there is 1 John 1:9: "If we confess our sins, he is faithful and just, and will forgive our sins and cleanse us from all unrighteousness." But we do not rely only on proof texts, when we have the whole New Testament with its record of the saving acts of God. Christ himself is God's great promise that he will forgive.

Pardon is one of the great words of the Bible. It is worth considering some of the figures of speech used in the Old Testament to bring out the perfection of God's forgiveness. "As far as the east is from the west, so far does he remove our transgressions from us" (Ps. 103:12). "Thou wilt cast all our sins into the depths of the sea" (Micah 7:19). "I will forgive their iniquity, and I will remember their sin no more" (Jer. 31:34). Truly, in the words of Isaiah 55:7, "he will abundantly pardon". In the New Testament we find St. John writing to the "little children, because your sins are forgiven for his sake" (1 John 2:12). It is clear that we are to experience forgiveness as a conscious certainty.

Pardon has to do with the past, but it leads to deliverance in the present. It is not God's purpose that we should be forgiven only to go back to the old sins. Of course, if we are relying on our own resolution that is exactly what will happen. But Christ's salvation is deliverance from sin's power as well as pardon of its guilty stain. Charles Wesley has put the two things magnificently into a single line:

He breaks the power of cancelled sin.

Yet we must not think of the Christian life only as deliverance from evil. This is the negative aspect. There is a positive side, being confirmed and strengthened in all goodness. Positive and negative are combined in St. Paul's words: "Put off your old nature which belongs to your former manner of life and is corrupt through deceitful lusts, and be renewed in the spirit of your minds, and put on the new nature, created after the likeness of God in true righteousness and holiness (Eph. 4:22-24). The goodness in which we are to be confirmed and strengthened is not a natural endowment but a gift of grace. It is that same grace that will keep us to the end and bring us to everlasting life. Our acceptance of all that the Absolution holds out to us is declared when we say *Amen*.

F

CHAPTER 13

THE COMFORTABLE WORDS

In Hermann's *Consultations* there were verses of Scripture between the Confession and Absolution, introduced by the words: "Hear the Gospel-comfort." Some of these were taken by our Reformers and placed *after* the Absolution, where they form the scriptural authority for the words just spoken. The term "Gospel-comfort" is in a sense more appropriate than *comfortable words*, in view of the change in the meaning of "comfortable" which we have already noticed. There is nothing soft about the Gospel, although there is abundant "encouragement (Authorised Version consolation) in Christ" (Phil. 2:1). The term *comfortable words* occurs in the introduction to the first two quotations, but they are taken to cover the other two as well, and are virtually the title of this section of the service. The comfortable words were in the 1549 Prayer Book, long before the Authorised Version of the Bible (1611). Hence the verbal differences, such as *travail* instead of "labour". Cranmer was using the Great Bible, which was largely the work of William Tyndale.

THE GREAT INVITATION

The first words of our Saviour Christ to those who truly turn to him were the only ones not among the Gospel-comfort in Hermann's work, though they were quoted by him in his preliminary discourse on the Lord's Supper. They come from St. Matthew 11:28, and are often referred to as the Great Invitation. The saying should of course be studied in its context, but even as quoted here, in isolation from what goes before and what follows, its message is clear. "Come unto me." In Isaiah 45:22 we have God saying: "Look unto me, and be-ye saved, all the ends of the earth" (A.V.). Here is Jesus saying, not, "Come unto God," but, "Come unto *me*." All his claims to be one with the Father are wrapped up in that invitation. The call is to *all that travail and are heavy laden.*

Perhaps our Lord was specially thinking of those who found the labour of trying to keep the Law too great a burden, or who were bowed down with a sense of sin, from which the religious practices of the Pharisees gave them no relief. But to all who find life to be travail, and who are weighed down with their sense of failure and inadequacy, the invitation is to come to him. He will refresh—give rest—by bringing the soul into fellowship with God through forgiveness. A quiet mind belongs to those who have received pardon and peace, and the cleansing of all their sins (Collect of Trinity XXI).

THE LOVE OF GOD

The second of the comfortable words is St. John 3 : 16, probably the best known words in the whole Bible, sometimes known as the Gospel in Miniature. As the Prayer Book stands, the words are attributed to our Lord himself, while many scholars (including Bishop Westcott) think that his conversation with Nicodemus ended at verse 15, and that what follows is St. John's inspired comment. But as A. J. Macleod says : "It is unquestionable that the evangelist has entered deeply into the mind of Jesus, and, if these are not his *ipsissima verba*, they certainly contain the very heart of the glorious evangel."[1]

No tender invitation to come to Jesus would be of any avail to the weary and heavy laden if it were not for the truths enshrined in this second word. It tells of the love of God for the world, of what that love was prepared to do for the world's salvation, and of the eternal consequences for those who believe. And while the results of faith in Christ endure into the world beyond, they begin here and now, for eternal life is represented, more particularly in St. John's Gospel, as a present possession.

[1] *The New Bible Commentary* (I.V.F.) p. 872.

A SAVIOUR FOR SINNERS

The third word is from St. Paul. The elementary fact of the Gospel is that *Christ Jesus came into the world to save sinners.* It would seem that this was one of the sayings taught to converts preparing for Baptism, or perhaps a watchword passed round among Christians. St. Paul could add his testimony to this. It is a *true* saying. Further, it applied to *all men*, and it is to be commended earnestly to their acceptance. The apostle knows that Christ came to save sinners, for he had saved the one who, in his own estimation at any rate, was the chief sinner of all. After the heart-searching of the Communion Service we may feel inclined to dispute St. Paul's right to his place as the chief of sinners. Many have learned to say with Wesley:

> *Can my Lord his wrath forbear,*
> *Me, the chief of sinners, spare?*

and the answer is YES. For this very purpose Christ Jesus came into the world.

OUR ADVOCATE

The final word is from St. John. He wrote his first Epistle to show the way of victory over sin. "My little children, I am writing this to you so that you may not sin" (1 John 2:1). But in this fallen world even the greatest saint knows that he is not perfect. Indeed, the greater the saint, the more conscious he is of imperfection. It is very immature Christians who sometimes think that there is not much wrong with them! So St. John tells of the provision God has made when we sin. *We have an Advocate with the Father, Jesus Christ the righteous.* In the Gospel of St. John the word here translated "Advocate" is rendered "Comforter", and is used of the Holy Spirit. It means literally "one who is called alongside". Jesus Christ stands with us, pleading our cause. We cannot plead our own, for we are unrighteous, but he is "the Righteous". Nor is that all. The one who pleads for us is the very same who died for us. This is quite stupendous. *He is the propitiation for our sins,* i.e. the one whose offering of himself effects our reconciliation with God.

We have said that the comfortable words can stand just as they are, apart from their context in the Bible. But in the case of the fourth it seems a pity that we must stop short at *he is the propitiation for our sins.* For the very next words in St. John's Epistle are "and not for ours only but also for the sins of the whole world". When you come to think of it, the Good News contained in the comfortable words is something which you cannot possibly enjoy selfishly. It is true for all men, everywhere. There is not one person in the world who is travailing and heavy laden whom Jesus does not include in his invitation. God so loved *the world.* The only people Christ did not come to save are those who are not sinners: and where are they? His death is for our sins—yes, for *my* sins—but not for ours only. To rejoice in the Gospel-comfort is to increase our missionary obligations many-fold.

CHAPTER 14

LIFT UP YOUR HEARTS

THERE is a very noticeable change in the tone of the service at this point. At the Invitation and Confession there is a sense of solemnity and unworthiness, based on the aweful holiness of God. With the Absolution and the Comfortable Words comes a lifting of the burden. There is happiness, even light-heartedness, about the ancient greeting *Sursum corda*: *Lift up your hearts*. The response of the people shows precisely what it means: *We lift them up unto the Lord*. There is here no cheap and easy encouragement to cheer up. It is rather a call, as those who are no longer burdened with the guilt of their sins, to "seek the things that are above" (Col. 3:1).

There is a time to look in, and a time to look up. Continual self-examination can lead to a morbid state. With the assurance of God's pardon we lift our hearts to him to prepare, in forget-fulness of self, to offer our adoration. In the city of Warsaw there is a remarkable statue outside the Church of the Holy Cross. It depicts our Lord, crowned with thorns, bearing his Cross on the road to Calvary. He is looking down on the people in the street below, and with one hand he is pointing upwards. Beneath the statue are the words *Sursum corda*. It is because he bore the Cross for us that we can lift up our hearts to him.

This versicle and response has been used at the Holy Com-munion at least since the third century, being mentioned by Cyprian, Bishop of Carthage, who was martyred in 258. Nor was it known only in one part of the Church, for Cyril, Bishop of Jerusalem in the fourth century, mentions it also. Not only do we value the use of words which have been tested over long centuries and link us with the early Church, but we are also glad that our Reformers retained the dialogue form. When

84

a response is called for, it means that the people are bound to take part. This is even more marked in Morning and Evening Prayer, and it may truly be said that Anglican worship is more congregational than many Free Church services.

The second versicle and response leads our up-lifted hearts to thanksgiving. It is a neglected duty. There are times when the heart is filled with happiness, and thanksgiving to God seems easy. But it is not to be reserved for occasions when we feel like it. Thanksgiving is a *duty*. *It is meet and right so to do*. In the regular worship of the Church there may be inadequate provision for this, and there is everything to be said for regular use of the General Thanksgiving. Its use also in private prayer has much to commend it. Until we learn to be more spontaneous in the continual giving of thanks, let us cling to the fact that our duty to God demands it. The Catechism says: "My duty towards God is . . . to give him thanks."

THE SANCTUS

The celebrant has now ceased to address the people, and so returns to his former position at the Lord's Table. He is now addressing God, and saying that *it is ver(il)y meet, right, and our bounden duty* to give thanks *at all times, and in all places*. This is thoroughly scriptural. "I will bless the Lord *at all times* : his praise shall continually be in my mouth" (Ps. 34:1). "Bless the Lord, all his works, *in all places* of his dominion" (Ps. 103:22). This obligation need not exclude special times and places for thanksgiving, and the custom of giving thanks at the meal table is one to be encouraged among Christian people. And now we have reached a moment in the service which is to be a special occasion of praise and adoration.

Therefore—because it is our bounden duty—*we laud and magnify thy glorious Name*. This, after all, is what we were created for, "to glorify God and to enjoy him for ever". But we do not do it alone. We are part of the whole Church, and in this most sacred activity we join *with Angels and Archangels, and with all the company of heaven*. They are doing it per-

fectly and continually; we worship imperfectly and intermit-
tently. We are momentarily anticipating the consummation of
all things, when we shall join eternally in the anthem: "Blessing and glory and wisdom and thanksgiving and honour and
power and might be to our God for ever and ever! Amen"
(Rev. 7:12). And even so we must remember that, unlike the
Angels, we can only be there as those who "have washed their
robes and made them white in the blood of the Lamb" (Rev.
7:14).

Though there is no rubrical direction, it is usual for the
whole congregation to join in at the words *Holy, holy, holy* . . .
In some churches the people begin at the word *Therefore*
. . . This part of the service, known as the *Sanctus*, is a hymn
of very early origin, based on the prophet's vision in Isaiah 6.
To the prophet the thrice repeated "Holy" was a solemn reminder of the "otherness" of God. He cannot have understood
it as implying the Trinity. As George Adam Smith says: "Their
thrice-uttered *Holy* is not theological accuracy, but religious
emphasis."[1] To us, on the other hand, it speaks unmistakably of
the glory of the triune God. He is the Lord of hosts: the King
of angels and of man. Isaiah says the whole earth is full of
his glory, and in the *Sanctus* we add that heaven, as well as
earth, are so filled, a fact which is almost taken for granted
in the prophetic vision.

When we ascribe glory to the Lord most High we are not
adding anything to the glory which is his already. He is already
all in all, and nothing we can do will increase the glory which
is complete. But we are called upon to acknowledge his
supremacy, to glorify him by accepting his kingly reign. To
say the words of the *Sanctus* with meaning we must bring
everything into subjection to the thrice holy Lord.

[1] *The Book of Isaiah* (Hodder and Stoughton) p. 66.

THE PROPER PREFACES

THE *Sanctus* is pure worship. But we can only worship a God whom we know, who has revealed himself to us. This revelation is given in Jesus Christ. The Gospel is not an ideology, but a series of historic facts. These are the facts in which we have professed our belief when we said the Nicene Creed. The same facts are commemorated in the Church's Year, that blessed safeguard against a lopsided presentation of the Gospel. Year by year, from Advent to Whitsun, we have brought before us the saving acts of God. The Incarnation, the Death and Resurrection, the Ascension of our Lord, and the coming of the Holy Ghost are the salient points, which bring us to the worship of the Holy and Undivided Trinity. So, in the Church's Year, Christmas Day, Easter Day, Ascension Day, Whitsunday and Trinity Sunday stand out as of special importance. For these a Proper Preface is provided, introducing a particular reason for the worship of the *Sanctus*. We may think of a number of other days for which a Proper Preface would be suitable, but reflection will show the wisdom of concentration on the greater crises in the drama of redemption.

CHRISTMAS

The first is to be said upon Christmas Day, and seven days after. Great festivals are continued for a week, which is known as an Octave. In mediaeval times many Saints' Days had Octaves, but even the Roman Church has now returned to their observance at the Great Feasts only. For the week which begins on Christmas Day we give thanks for the birth of Jesus Christ *as at this time for us*. He is God's eternal Son, begotten not made. He was born in time, on a given date at a given place. All birth is mysterious and wonderful: this birth was unique. Never before or since has the Word become flesh and dwelt among us. Such a unique event was brought about in a unique manner, *by the operation of the Holy Ghost*. Yet the child who was born was not a being unlike other humans. As to his body, soul and spirit he *was made ver(il)y man of the substance of the Virgin Mary his mother*. This truth is most clearly set forth in Article II.

Article XV declares: "Christ in the truth of our nature was made like unto us in all things, sin only except, from which he was clearly void, both in his flesh, and in his spirit." He was born into the world *without spot of sin*. In this he was absolutely alone. The Roman Church teaches that our Lord's Mother was also without sin, that "from the first moment of her conception the Blessed Virgin Mary was, by the singular grace and privilege of Almighty God, and in view of the merits of Jesus Christ, Saviour of mankind, kept free from all stain of original sin" (the Papal Bull of 1854 defining the dogma of the Immaculate Conception). There is nothing in Scripture to support such a view. Yet, while we repudiate every tendency to exalt the Mother of Our Lord to a place she is not given in Scripture, we do well to remember the position of unique privilege given to her, and her own words, "For behold, henceforth all generations will call me blessed" (Luke 1:48).

The purpose of the Incarnation must be kept to the fore in our commemoration of the event of the Virgin Birth. It is not just a lovely story unrelated to the plan of salvation. We have already seen that Christ Jesus came into the world to save sinners. The sinless Saviour was born *to make us clean from all sin*. It was the first step in the humbling which culminated at the Cross. We give thanks for Jesus Christ, "who gave himself for us to redeem us from all iniquity and to purify for himself a people of his own who are zealous for good deeds" (Titus 2:14). This was the message of the angel: "She will bear a son, and you shall call his name Jesus, for he will save his people from their sins" (Matt. 1:21).

EASTER

The second of the Proper Prefaces is said upon Easter Day, and seven days after. At no time of the year is the reminder of the Octave more needed. Easter Sunday being a high festival, there is a tendency for Low Sunday to be an anti-climax. The truth is that both Sundays are within the Easter Festival, and Low Sunday ought to be a triumphant ending to the week. Even when we have said that, we need to remember that every Sunday is a lesser Easter, a weekly reminder of the Lord's Resurrection.

The words *But chiefly* which introduce this Preface are more than a way of calling attention to the fact that it is Easter. The Resurrection is always the chief cause of our praise, for "if Christ has not been raised, your faith is futile and you are still in your sins" (1 Cor. 15:17). His Resurrection is indeed *glorious*, and nowhere are the results of it more succinctly put than in this Preface. As the Passover Lamb was slain for the redemption of Israel, so Christ was offered. In the words of John the Baptist: "Behold, the Lamb of God, who takes away the sin of the world" (John 1:29). The Resurrection proclaims to us the certainty of our redemption. As, at the Passover, Israel escaped from death and slavery, so in the Resurrection we learn of the destruction of death and the restoring to us of everlasting life.

Something of the joy of Easter is reflected in the story of Christian losing his burden in Bunyan's *Pilgrim's Progress*. "He ran thus till he came to a place somewhat ascending, and upon that place stood a Cross, and a little below in the bottom, a Sepulchre. So I saw in my Dream, that just as Christian came up with the Cross, his Burden loosed from off his shoulders, and fell from off his back, and began to tumble, and so continued to do, till it came to the mouth of the Sepulchre, where it fell in, and I saw it no more ... Then was Christian glad and lightsome, and said with a merry heart, He hath given me rest by his sorrow, and life by his death."

THE ASCENSION

Christmas and Easter are historic facts which happened once and for ever in time. The Ascension is the beginning of the Heavenly Session, and we think of Christ ever living to make intercession for us. Similarly on Whitsunday the Holy Spirit was given to abide with the Church for ever. [1]Cosslett Quin, in pointing out that both these occasions were the beginning of a work which still continues, shows the appropriateness of the preposition "through" with which the two Proper Prefaces begin. While this is true and helpful, we need not lose sight of the actual events of the Ascension and Pentecost. The Prayer Book seems to stress this. Our Lord, after the Resurrection, *manifestly appeared to all his Apostles, and in their sight ascended up into heaven.*

The ascended Christ is the forerunner. He had promised: "I go to prepare a place for you" (John 14:2). In the Preface the emphasis is on the believer's ultimate entry into heaven to reign with Christ in glory. The Collect of Ascension Day prays that we may "in heart and mind thither ascend, and with him continually dwell". St. Paul teaches that because of the believer's union with Christ, "you have died, and your life is hid with Christ in God" (Col. 3:3). By virtue of our identification with the ascended Lord we are already made to "sit with him in the heavenly places in Christ Jesus" (Eph. 2:6).

WHITSUNDAY

The Whitsunday Preface is to be said on *six* days after, as the seventh day is Trinity Sunday, with a special message of its own. The events of the Day of Pentecost are brought before us in detail: the sound of the mighty wind, the appearance of the fiery tongues, the gift of divers languages. These were the accompaniments of the giving of the Spirit. The outward signs vanish, but the Gift remains. He was given to teach. "But the Counsellor, the Holy Spirit, whom the Father will send in my

[1] *At the Lord's Table* (Lutterworth Press), p. 160.

name, he will teach you all things, and bring to your remembrance all that I have said to you" (John 14:26). "When the Spirit of truth comes, he will guide you into all the truth" (John 16:13). It is through the fulfilment of these promises that we have the New Testament, and the same Holy Spirit guides us in our interpretation of it.

The Holy Spirit was given, not only that we should understand the truth, but also that we might propagate it. Whatever the precise meaning of speaking with tongues—and what happened on the Day of Pentecost does not seem to be quite the same as what St. Paul refers to in 1 Corinthians 14—the lesson for us is plain. The Gospel is to be preached to the people of all nations in their own language. The slackness of the Church in doing this is a measure of our neglect of the Holy Spirit. It is he who gives the *boldness* and the *fervent zeal* to do this, and the perseverance to do it *constantly*. It is because someone was stirred by the Spirit to preach the Gospel on these shores that *we* have been brought from darkness to light. Common decency would suggest that we in our turn should tell others, but it takes the power of Pentecost to make us into missionaries.

TRINITY SUNDAY

The final Preface is upon the Feast of Trinity only. All the year round we worship the Three in One and One in Three. But one special day is set apart to emphasise the doctrine of the Trinity. It is the day for trying, not to explain, but to contemplate, the mystery of God. The Trinity is not a puzzle to be solved, but a revelation to be received. Ultimately we find the meaning of our existence, and of the world in which we live, in the worship of Almighty God. The Athanasian Creed is the Church's greatest expression of the doctrine of God. And it begins, not with the affirmation "I believe", but with the statement "we worship". "The Catholick Faith is this: That *we worship* one God in Trinity, and Trinity in Unity." It is perhaps well that the Reformers saw fit to shorten the more complicated Preface in the Sarum Missal. The simple statement of the equality of the three Persons is such as every worshipper can grasp. This, with the omission of the words "Holy Father" in the introduction to the *Sanctus*, teaches the fact of the Three in One.

The rubric after the Prefaces directs that what follows shall be sung or said. The choice is partly a matter of temperament, but even more of custom. We grow up with the notion that the way things are done in our church is the right way. There need be no prejudice against using music in our highest moments of adoration, especially when the Prayer Book suggests it. Our Lord and his disciples sang a hymn (the Great Hallel)[1] at the Last Supper, and the singing of the *Sanctus* can be of great devotional value. This is not to undervalue the saying of it, slowly and reverently, which is equally rubrical.

[1] See page 119.

CHAPTER 16

THE PRAYER OF HUMBLE ACCESS

Then shall the Priest, kneeling down at the Lord's Table, say . . .
We have just been joining with Angels and Archangels, and
all the company of heaven, in adoration of the thrice holy God.
It is by grace alone that we find ourselves in this exalted fellowship of worshippers. We must never for one moment think
of ourselves as fit to stand before God in any righteousness of
our own. We sometimes sing:

> *Not for our sins alone*
> *Thy mercy, Lord, we sue;*
> *Let fall thy pitying glance*
> *On our devotions too,*
> *What we have done for thee,*
> *And what we think to do.*
>
> *The holiest hours we spend*
> *In prayer upon our knees,*
> *The times when most we deem*
> *Our songs of praise will please,*
> *Thou searcher of all hearts,*
> *Forgiveness pour on these.*

This is good, but it does not go far enough. It may give the
impression that our worship merely falls short of what it ought
to be, and therefore needs God's forgiveness. The simple truth
is that we have no right to appear before God at all in ourselves. Says Bishop Stephen Neill: "Much popular theology and
Christian devotion is based on the idea, not clearly expressed
but unmistakably revealed by careful analysis, that some day,

perhaps not in this world and only after long purgation, we shall reach a condition in which God will be able to approve of us as we are in ourselves. This is a fatal theological error . . . A time will never come when we shall be able to depend on our own righteousness as that which can commend us to God. To the end of all eternity, the highest situation to which we can aspire is that which already we have, that of sinners saved by grace."[1]

There is no mistaking the intention of the compilers of the Prayer Book. For the second time in the service the celebrant kneels. As at the General Confession, so now, he is in the position of complete dependence on the mercy of God. To come trusting in any supposed righteousness of our own is the height of presumption. "All our righteous deeds are like a polluted garment" (Isaiah 64:6). We cannot stand before God in the filthy rags of our own goodness. What then is our plea?

> *Just as I am*, without one plea,
> *But that thy blood was shed for me,*
> *And that thou bidst me come to thee,*
> *O Lamb of God, I come.*

We trust in his *manifold and great mercies.*

Our unworthiness is described in strong pictorial terms. We are not fit to gather the crumbs under the Table. The words are reminiscent of the Syrophoenician woman in Mark 7:28, who spoke about the dogs under the table eating the children's crumbs. Far from being children who have a *right*, we are not even like the dogs who come uninvited to eat what may fall. But this is not how God treats us. As David showed mercy to Mephibosheth, a grandson of his old enemy, so the Lord shows mercy to us. "So Mephibosheth ate at David's table, like one of the king's sons" (2 Sam. 9:11). He is *the same Lord whose property is always to have mercy.* Mercy belongs to his character.

[1] The Triumph of God (Longman's, Green), p. 24.

EATING AND DRINKING BY FAITH

We are allowed, by God's amazing grace, to come to the Feast. Shall we profit by it? The Bread of Life is there for all to receive, as the Word of Life is for all to hear. Yet there were those of whom it had to be said: "But the message which they heard did not benefit them, because it did not meet with faith in the hearers" (Heb. 4:2). It is the same with the Sacrament. "The Wicked, and such as be void of a lively faith, although they do carnally and visibly press with their teeth (as Saint Augustine saith) the Sacrament of the Body and Blood of Christ, yet in no wise are they partakers of Christ" (Article XXIX). Great emphasis is laid on the need of faith. "The mean whereby the Body of Christ is received and eaten in the Supper is Faith" (Article XXVIII).

If we so eat the flesh of the Son of God, and drink His blood, certain results will follow. Jesus said: "He who eats my flesh and drinks my blood has eternal life, and I will raise him up at the last day. For my flesh is food indeed, and my blood is drink indeed. He who eats my flesh and drinks my blood abides in me, and I in him" (John 6:54-56). We become partakers in Christ's Death and Resurrection, united to him by grace through faith. This brings cleansing, renewal, the continual abiding of Christ in us, and we in him. All this is to become real to us at the Lord's Table.

> Here to learn through hallowed symbol
> What thy grace for all can be,
> By that wonderful indwelling—
> Thou in us, and we in thee.

One result of the Reformation was the restoring of the cup to the laity. The practice of intinction, where the bread is dipped in the wine and the two are administered together, is merely an expedient for dealing with infectious cases of sickness. We should normally take the bread and wine separately, as our Lord's precious blood was separated from his body on

G

the Cross. It is however going rather far in speculation to associate two different results with the bread and the wine. This is what this prayer seems to do, and we may prefer to combine the two thoughts in our minds. Our souls and bodies, both, are cleansed and renewed by the body and blood of Christ.

Are we right at all in bringing the body into such a spiritual thing as salvation? Of course, spiritual cleansing is not to be a substitute for what can be done with "pure water" (Heb. 10:22), though the reference here is probably to Baptism. Devotional exercises are not to take the place of "bodily training [which] is of some value" (1 Tim. 4:8). The medicine of the soul need not exclude the use of medicine for the body. Yet the interplay of body, mind and spirit is so intimate that the three cannot be divided. The body is often the cause of temptation and sin. As we have seen in an earlier chapter, spiritual disharmony is a fruitful cause of bodily illness. In asking that our bodies be made clean and our souls washed we are praying for *wholeness*, which is almost a synonym of holiness.

CHAPTER 17

THE PRAYER OF CONSECRATION

THE celebrant has been on his knees to say, in the name of all the communicants, the Prayer of Humble Access. He now rises to his feet and so orders the bread and wine, *that he may with the more readiness and decency break the Bread before the people, and take the Cup into his hands.* While he does this he will be *standing before the Table.* It seems clear from the history of the rubric that this direction was to prevent the unseemliness of the celebrant leaning over from the north side to reach the vessels in the centre of a large Communion Table. The Prayer Book, in the Preface "Concerning Ceremonies", quotes: *"Let all things be done among you,* saith St. Paul, *in a seemly and due order."* An intense regard for reverence is part of the genius of Anglican worship.

The other point to be noted from this rubric is that the Priest is to break the bread *before the people.* When Archbishop Benson gave his decision in the Lincoln Judgment (1889-1892) that the eastward position was not illegal, he insisted that the manual acts must be visible to the people. Considerable use was made of the phrase *standing before the Table* to show that it was at least permissible for the celebrant to stand facing east during the Prayer of Consecration. The expression had previously been interpreted as applying only to his position while he *ordered the Bread and Wine.* The Church of Ireland Prayer Book has removed all ambiguity by inserting in the rubric *he shall, standing at the north side of the Table, say the Prayer of Consecration.*

Controversy in matters connected with this most sacred service is distasteful. To argue over the legality of this or that practice, or to appeal to the happenings of a century ago, seems quite irrelevant to the Church fighting for the souls of men today. But reality and reverence in devotion, and truth and consistency in doctrine, are always to be maintained. Hence it is not unimportant to emphasise the directions of the rubric that all should be done decently and in order, and that the breaking of the bread should be done *before the people*. In the action done, as well as in the words said, all are to see and hear the proclamation of the Lord's death.

The Prayer of Consecration as we now have it dates from the second Prayer Book of Edward VI (1552). A comparison of it with that in the first Prayer Book (1549) shows how the Reformers were moving even further away from the mediaeval doctrine of "the sacrifices of Masses, in the which it was commonly said, that the Priest did offer Christ for the quick and the dead, to have remission of pain or guilt" (Article XXXI). Chiefly significant is the omission of the *epiclesis* (invocation of the Holy Spirit upon the elements), and of the *anamnesis* (the memorial *before God* of the Lord's death "with these thy holy gifts").

The Prayer is in three parts. The first contains a statement of the fact of the atoning death of Christ, and the relation of the Sacrament to it; the second, a prayer that those who receive the bread and wine may be partakers of Christ's Body and Blood; the third, a recital, with the appropriate actions, of the events in the Upper Room on the night of the Institution.

THE ATONEMENT

First, then, we find the fact of the Atonement clearly stated. The statement is contained in a series of relative clauses following the address to *Almighty God, our heavenly Father*. We note that the redemption of the world originated in the loving heart of God. Neither Scripture nor Prayer Book countenances for one moment the notion of a loving Jesus saving mankind from the wrath of an offended God. It was the Father himself who of his *tender mercy . . . gave* his Son. We have seen this already in the second of the Comfortable Words. Yet the Son also gave himself when "He humbled himself and became obedient unto death, even death on a cross" (Phil. 2:8). This mighty act of God was *for our redemption*. "In him we have redemption through his blood, the forgiveness of our trespasses, according to the riches of his grace which he lavished upon us" (Eph. 1:7, 8).

In a further subordinate clause we learn in greater detail of the fulness of the divine provision. It was *by his one oblation of himself once offered*. The Jewish priests needed "to offer sacrifice daily, first for his own sins, and then for those of the people; but he [Jesus] did this once for all when he offered up himself" (Heb. 7:27). "He has appeared once for all at the end of the age to put away sin by the sacrifice of himself" (Heb. 9:26). His was the sacrifice to end all other sacrifices for sin. And he made the sacrifice *there*, on the Cross. On a given date, at a place called Calvary, the deed was done which brought salvation. There can never be a repetition of what happened once and for all on the first Good Friday. This the Reformers were at pains to stress, for the teaching they repudiated was that, in the Mass, Christ was offered again, his sacrifice repeated.

Word after word piles up to stress the completeness of the finished work of Christ. It is called a *sacrifice*, linking the Cross with the idea of propitiation; an *oblation*, with the thought of Christ's voluntary self-offering; and a *satisfaction*, referring to our Lord's paying the ransom price to set men free. (See Mark 10:45.) The three adjectives preceding these words all apply to the three nouns, though they may each have a special application to one of them. Thus we may see that the sacrifice was *full*, making complete atonement for all our sins. The oblation was *perfect*; he poured out his life to the uttermost; there was nothing lacking in his offering. The satisfaction was *sufficient*; the debt was paid to the last farthing. And all this was *for the sins of the whole world*. In some memorable words of Douglas Webster: "Every human being in the whole world is a died-for person."[1]

[1] *Into All the World* (S.P.C.K.) p. 8.

THE PERPETUAL MEMORY

No less clearly is it stated that our Lord instituted *a perpetual memory of that his precious death, until his coming again.* While the earlier service of 1549 did not omit this aspect of the Sacrament, it also included the making of a memorial before God. From 1552 to the present time our Prayer Book has omitted the latter from its liturgy. In doing so it emphasises the completeness of the once-and-for-all sacrifice of Calvary. The re-introduction of the 1549 doctrine in the Deposited Book of 1928 was one of the main reasons for the strenuous opposition to it. The question at issue is ultimately whether in the Eucharist we are offering Christ to the Father, or the Father is offering Christ to us. By reason of its brevity, that is an inadequate statement of the case, but it will serve to bring out the contrast. On this question Bishop Stephen Neill has said: "It is impossible to pretend that these two views, even stated moderately, are ultimately reconcilable, as different emphases within a common understanding. They do depend on very deep differences in belief as to the nature of God and of his action in the world."[1]

This perpetual memory, a constant reminder to the Church of the sacrifice of the Cross and a means whereby we receive the benefits of his passion, our Saviour has commanded us to continue *until his coming again.* The expectation of the Second Advent runs through the whole New Testament, giving a sense of urgency to the call to holiness. The promise is that "when he appears we shall be like him, for we shall see him as he is" (1 John 3:2). When that day comes we shall no longer stand in need of Sacraments. Till that time we are to remember him in the way he has appointed. He has so commanded us *in his holy Gospel.*

The second part of the Prayer of Consecration is a single petition that we who receive the bread and wine may be partakers of Christ's Body and Blood. What we receive is described as *these thy creatures of bread and wine.* This, as the Catechism

[1] *The Holy Communion: A Symposium* (S.C.M.) p. 65.

puts it, is "the outward part or sign of the Lord's Supper". God's *creatures*, or created things, are "Bread and Wine, which the Lord hath commanded to be received" (Catechism). The Prayer Book is very careful to guard against the doctrine of a change in the substance of the elements. "Transubstantiation [or the change of the substance of bread and wine] in the Supper of the Lord, cannot be proved by holy Writ; but is repugnant to the plain words of Scripture" (Article XXVIII). Indeed, the Church goes further, and says in Article XXIX that those who receive the Sacrament of the Body and Blood of Christ without repentance and faith are in no wise partakers of Christ. But equally certainly, the inward part of the Sacrament is "the Body and Blood of Christ, *which are verily and indeed taken and received by the faithful* in the Lord's Supper".

THE INSTITUTION RECALLED

We pass to the third part of the Prayer of Consecration, which is a recital of the account of the Institution, accompanied by the appropriate manual acts. If the congregation is to say an intelligent *Amen* to what is done, as well as what is said, they should keep their eyes open for this part of the prayer. The actions of the upper room are pieced together from the accounts in the Synoptic Gospels and in 1 Corinthians 11. By faith we see, not a human Minister, but the Lord himself, presiding at his Table. We are there with him *in the same night that he was betrayed*. It is wonderful that he chose that moment, when sin was about to show itself at its very worst, to reveal his eternal love in this way.

First he took *bread*. He does it even now, as *Here the Priest is to take the Paten into his hands*. As we watch, we remember that it is the Lord who takes the bread and will presently give it to us. "*And when he had given thanks, he brake it.*" The appropriate action is *And here to break the Bread*. Thanksgiving is a way of consecrating anything. At a meal, we "give thanks", or "ask a blessing", or "say grace", and they all mean the same thing. The breaking of the bread is such an essential part that the expression came to be used for the entire service. We are doing exactly what our Lord did on that first night. *He brake it, and gave it to his disciples.* The broken bread is given. It was as he gave it to them that he said: *Take, eat, this is my Body, which is given for you.* The rubric, *And here to lay his hand upon all the Bread,* directs the appropriate manual act to accompany these words. By the laying on of the hand that bread is now separated, or set apart, for a sacred purpose.

It is important to note that what we think of as words of consecration are, in a sense, words of administration. Without the *giving* of the bread to the communicants, it cannot be said to be really consecrated. The words, *Do this in remembrance of me,* refer to the whole action of the Communion, including *Take, eat.* The same applies to the consecration of the wine. *Likewise after supper he took the cup.* For centuries before the Reformation the cup had been denied to the laity. But our Lord, at the Institution, *gave it to them saying, Drink ye all of this.* The Revised Standard Version removes any possible misunderstanding of these words from St. Matthew's Gospel: "Drink of it, all of you" (Matt. 26:27). The Reformers gave back to the laity the Sacrament as our Lord instituted it.

The rubrics about the cup are self-explanatory. Be it noted that the provision for consecrating the wine in the flagon as well as in the chalice is more frequently required in these days when the Parish Communion is bringing larger numbers to the Lord's Table. The words said for the cup are: *This is my Blood of the New Testament.* The word *testament* here means covenant. The old Covenant was sealed with the blood of animal sacrifices (Ex. 24:8). The new Covenant, promised as long ago as Jeremiah 31:31-34, was sealed with the Blood of Christ. (See Heb. 9:15-28.) The New Testament is a Covenant of grace, *for the remission of sins.* And it is made, not with a nation, but with all who believe. Christ's Blood was shed *for you and for many.* Every Communion Service should remind us of all for whom Christ died, including those who have never heard, the "other sheep" of John 10:16.

CHAPTER 18

THE ADMINISTRATION

Then shall the Minister first receive the Communion in both kinds himself. It is interesting that the word *Minister* should be chosen here : it emphasises that the celebrant is the servant of the people. Before he can administer the Sacrament to others, he must receive it himself. This is a parable of the whole of a Minister's life : he can only lead others where he himself has been. Having received the Communion, he will *then proceed to deliver the same to the Bishops, Priests, and Deacons, in like manner (if any be present).* This is simply, as earlier versions of the rubric expressed it, "that they may be ready to help the chief Minister". If a Bishop, or any other Minister, is present *in the congregation,* he comes up in his turn with all the rest. We are all equal at the Lord's Table.

And after that to the people also in order. When a large number of communicants is present it is seemly that there shall be some ordering, possibly by a sidesman, of their coming forward. This is better than an unorganised queue, or alternatively an over literal obedience to St. Paul's injunction to "wait for one another" (1 Cor. 11 : 33). Either before or after receiving, according to whether we are among the first or the last to come up, there is precious time for meditation and prayer. Since it is a *Communion,* and not an act of individual worship, it is well to bring our fellow communicants into our prayers. Care should be taken to observe whatever customs prevail in the particular church about kneeling at the rail. There are churches where no one rises until all who are kneeling at one time have partaken. In most churches each communicant rises when he or she has received the wine, always allowing a moment so as not to disturb the person next receiving.

. . . into their hands, all meekly kneeling. In the first Prayer Book (1549) the then existing custom was retained, and the people were to receive the Sacrament in their mouths, at the Priest's hand. There was a note to the effect that the older use was to receive "in their own hands"; but some had "conveyed the same secretly away, kept it with them, and diversely abased it to superstition and wickedness". By 1552 the Reformers evidently thought that there was no further danger of this abuse, and they reverted to the more primitive use. *Kneeling* is a mark of reverence and humility. Puritan objection to it, on the ground that it implied adoration of the sacramental bread and wine, is dealt with in the final rubric at the end of the service. While it is not expressly stated that the Minister should himself receive kneeling, it would seem to be most fitting. Sometimes the Minister actually says the words of administration aloud to himself, changing *thee* to *me*, *thy* to *my*, and inserting the word *I* before *take*. More often he will say the words mentally. The congregation should pray for their Minister at this point.

THE WORDS OF ADMINISTRATION

The Words of Administration have a history which throws light on their meaning. In the first Prayer Book, the first half only of our present words are found. These were taken from an older form, but with the significant addition of the words, *which was given for thee*. This really had the effect of concentrating the mind on the historic fact of the sacrifice of Calvary, where Christ's Body *was given*. But those who clung to a too close association of the sacramental bread with the material Body of Christ found that they could still read this meaning into the words. Accordingly, in the second Prayer Book (1552) the words were completely changed, and our present second half was substituted. But a study of this shows that it *could* be interpreted to mean that we do no more than take and eat bread in remembrance of Christ's death. This is the doctrine associated with Zwingli.

At a time like the Reformation there was bound to be confusion of thought and of language. A great battle was being fought to bring the Church to conformity with the doctrine of Holy Scripture. In the judgment of the English Reformers the New Testament taught neither Transubstantiation on the one hand, nor a merely memorialist view on the other. The Anglican position is contained in the words: "The Body and Blood of Christ, which are verily and indeed taken and received by the faithful in the Lord's Supper" (Catechism). Now if the 1549 words were capable of being understood to imply Transubstantiation (though most would deny this), and if the 1552 words were thought to betoken Zwinglianism (though this need not be the case), what was to be done? The answer was found in the Elizabethan Settlement of 1559, when the two sets of words were combined. Thus each safeguards the other from possible misunderstanding.

It must be admitted that the Words of Administration as we now have them are over-long if they are repeated in full to each communicant. A common custom, which has much to commend it, is to say the words to two communicants at a time, in such a way that both hear the whole. This is preferable to the habit of using only one half of the words. With the growing appreciation of the corporate nature of the Sacrament, it might be considered whether the words could be said once, for all who are kneeling at the rail at the same time. One can see the value of this, especially where, as in a few churches, the communicants kneel at a rail which surrounds the Holy Table. This is fellowship indeed, and we might well revive the custom, if not the phrase, of "saying the words for the Table".

CHRIST FOR US, AND IN US

In the Words of Administration we note that both the Body and Blood of Christ are associated with the preservation of both our body and soul unto everlasting life. This seems to correct a possible misconception which we saw in the Prayer of Humble Access. Christ's atoning death is for our abundant life.

While physical health is not by any means always granted to the faithful, we recognise the intimate connection between body and soul. Spiritual wholeness sometimes can do no more than supply the courage to bear physical suffering bravely. Yet the doctrine of the resurrection of the body, when that which is sown a physical body is raised a spiritual body (see 1 Cor. 15:44), teaches us that God has a purpose for our whole being which will find its fulfilment beyond this present world. To bring us to eternal life, Christ, the eternal Son of God, died.

Yet in the Words of Administration we are not only shown that we partake in the atoning death of Christ; we also feed on him in our hearts by faith. He is "the bread of life" (John 6:48), "the food which supplies life" (Westcott). He is also "the living bread" (John 6:51), who imparts and sustains eternal life because he possesses that life in himself. The victory of the Cross was followed inevitably by the vindication of the Resurrection, and it is the living Christ who is our sustenance.

"The Body of Christ is given, taken, and eaten, in the Supper, only after an heavenly and spiritual manner. And the mean whereby the Body of Christ is received and eaten in the Supper is Faith" (Article XXVIII). At the very moment of receiving, the communicant is bidden, *feed on him in thy heart by faith.* "Now faith is the assurance of things hoped for, the conviction of things not seen" (Heb. 11:1). By faith we know the indwelling of Christ in our hearts, not simply at a moment in the Communion Service, but as a continuing relationship. (See Eph. 3:17.) There can be but one response to our Lord's gift of himself to our faith, and that is thanksgiving. From now onwards this is the predominating note in the service. Having received the bread and wine we go back to our places to join in the Post-Communion in which we offer our sacrifice of praise.

In the rubric following the Words of Administration we have directions for consecrating more bread and wine as need may arise. It shows that, in the opinion of the Reformers, the essential part of consecration is the recital of the words of institu-

tion, with the accompanying manual acts. We are reminded of
the lines, attributed to Queen Elizabeth I:

> *His was the Word, he spake it,*
> *He took the Bread, and brake it,*
> *And what his Word doth make it,*
> *That I believe, and take it.*

That probably describes the experience of thousands of devout
souls, who ask no further explanation. A second rubric directs
the covering of *what remaineth of the consecrated Elements . . .*
with a fair linen cloth. No direction at all was given about this
until the present Prayer Book (1662), when it was thought
necessary to prevent any adoration being offered to the Sacramental Elements. It also shows the Anglican love of reverence
and order.

CHAPTER 19

THE SACRIFICE OF PRAISE

WE have noted that whenever in the Prayer Book the Lord's Prayer occurs without the Doxology, it is as an introduction to petition; where it concludes with *For thine is the kingdom, the power, and the glory, for ever and ever*, it introduces praise. At the beginning of the service we had the shorter form, said by the Priest alone, for reasons before suggested. Now we have the longer form, said by the Priest, *the people repeating after him every petition*. This is interpreted to mean all saying it together. It is a triumphant moment in the service when, all having been assured afresh of their calling as children of God, we join to say *Our Father*. In the 1549 service the Lord's Prayer was introduced with the words: "As our Saviour Christ hath commanded and taught us, we are bold to say"—and possibly we need some such preface so that we can all come in together at the opening words of the Lord's Prayer.

This is the beginning of our Thanksgiving, although in a sense the whole service is a Eucharist. In 1549 the Lord's Prayer came immediately after the long Prayer of Consecration which included the Prayer of Oblation. Following the Lord's Prayer were the Confession, Absolution, Comfortable Words and Prayer of Humble Access, and only then the Communion. From 1552 onwards all this comes before the Prayer of Consecration, which is followed immediately by the Communion. This emphasises that the sole purpose of the Consecration is that the Sacrament shall be *received*. It is *then* that we join in the great Family Prayer. With renewed faith we call God *Father*; with quickened love of the brethren we call him *our* Father.

Because it is the prayer which Jesus taught us we know that

108

we are asking according to God's will. Even as we say the words we know that he hears us. We repeat the prayer with confident and expectant faith, for we have seen Christ's victory, and been made one with it. As we ask for the hallowing of God's Name, the coming of his kingdom, the doing of his will, we are not asking the impossible. We have seen it as something which *must* happen because Christ has conquered. Even for our daily bread we ask with a new assurance when we have tasted of the Bread of Life. Forgiveness is a great reality, for we have seen our sins laid on Jesus. So we want to forgive others. And we are going forth by the leading of God, with a new strength to overcome every evil.

As we say the Lord's Prayer in this particular context it becomes more truly praise than petition. So we add the Doxology. The words are not a part of the original Greek text as recorded by St. Matthew. They were very early used as a liturgical ending, an echo of David's prayer in 1 Chron. 29:11. It is easy to see how some copyist wrote them in to a manuscript of St. Matthew that he was transcribing. They form a glorious, triumphant climax to the Lord's Prayer, leading us in to the praise and adoration that follows.

The Church is described as "a holy priesthood, to offer spiritual sacrifices acceptable to God through Jesus Christ" (1 Pet. 2:5). Our Lord alone is the great High Priest who "entered once for all into the Holy Place, taking . . . his own blood, thus securing an eternal redemption" (Heb. 9:12). The Church cannot add to his perfect sacrifice by which the world is redeemed. But as a priestly body the Church offers the sacrifice of praise and thanksgiving. St. Peter says again: "You are a chosen race, *a royal priesthood*, a holy nation, God's own people, that you may declare the wonderful deeds of him who called you out of darkness into his marvellous light" (1 Pet. 2:9).

> *Kings and priests, by God anointed,*
> *Shall ye not declare his grace?*

This is what we do in the Prayer of Oblation. This prayer is almost exactly the same as the ending of the Prayer of Consecration in 1549. Its removal in 1552 to its present place shows the Reformers' desire that there should be no confusion between the sacrifice of thanksgiving and what Article XXXI called "the sacrifices of Masses".

THE PRAYER OF OBLATION

Our position as Kings and Priests is altogether by God's grace. We are nothing in ourselves, apart from Christ. So we begin: *O Lord and heavenly Father, we thy humble servants entirely desire thy fatherly goodness mercifully to accept this our sacrifice of praise and thanksgiving.* It is still the language of a sinner, albeit a sinner saved by grace. The sinner's plea is *by the merits and death of thy Son Jesus Christ, and through faith in his Blood.* This latter phrase is taken from Romans 3:25 where we read of "the redemption which is in Christ Jesus, whom God put forward as an expiation by his blood, to be received by faith". The prayer is that *we and all thy whole Church may obtain remission of our sins, and all other benefits of his passion.* It is a prayer that we may experience all that God wills to give us in Christ.

One of the *benefits of his passion* is the privilege of being no longer our own. "You are not your own; you were bought with a price. So glorify God in your body" (1 Cor. 6:19, 20). It is, however, one thing to know that we belong to God, quite another to surrender our lives to him. Yet there is no sacrifice of praise and thanksgiving without the offering of the whole of our being to God. In the words of the General Thanksgiving, "We shew forth thy praise, not only with our lips, but in our lives; by giving up ourselves to thy service, and by walking before thee in holiness and righteousness all our days." St. Paul makes it the subject of earnest entreaty: "I appeal to you therefore, brethren, by the mercies of God, to present your bodies as a living sacrifice, holy and acceptable to God, which is your spiritual worship" (Rom. 12:1).

We note that the apostolic appeal is in virtue of all that has gone before in the Epistle to the Romans: *"therefore"*. Because of the mercies of God revealed in the Gospel, present your bodies. There is no good news in the saying, "Give yourself to God". The Good News is "God so loved the world that *he* gave". We are entirely at the receiving end. But, having received, we seek to give in return. The language of the redeemed soul is: "What shall I render to the Lord for all his bounty to me?" (Ps. 116:12). So, after giving thanks, we continue: *And here we offer and present unto thee, O Lord, ourselves, our souls and bodies.*

It is well that we specify that the offering of ourselves is a total sacrifice, and includes body as well as soul. To St. Paul the presenting of "your bodies as a living sacrifice" is what is "holy and acceptable to God". He knew the danger of a religion which was only mystical, divorced from everyday life. Surrender to God means giving him my head to think for him, my hands to work for him, my feet to go for him, my lips to speak for him. "Do you know that your body is a temple of the Holy Spirit within you, which you have from God" (1 Cor. 6:19)? "For we must all appear before the judgment seat of Christ, so that each one may receive good or evil, according to that which he has done *in the body*" (2 Cor. 5:10).

PRACTICAL IMPLICATIONS

The yielding of *ourselves, our souls and bodies* is *to be a reasonable, holy and lively sacrifice unto thee*. The language follows Romans 12:1 closely. "Reasonable service", as the Authorised Version translates, means (as J. B. Phillips puts it) "an act of intelligent worship". This is the only really *"spiritual worship"*. Emotional rapture which does not lead to obedience in daily life is definitely unspiritual, as well as unintelligent. The sacrifice is *holy* in the original sense of the word, something which is wholly dedicated to the Lord. There can be no holding back in making a complete surrender. This alone is "acceptable to God". And the sacrifice is also *lively*. We offer ourselves as those who in Christ have been "made alive" (Eph. 2:1). "Yield

H

yourselves to God as men who have been brought from death to life" (Rom. 6 : 13).

The outcome of the surrender for which St. Paul appeals in Romans 12 : 1 is to be a transformation from the life of worldliness to the life of obedience to the will of God. This is not achieved by our own unaided effort, but "by the renewal of your mind" (Romans 12 : 2). Our act of surrender simply removes the barriers we set up against the working of God's grace. "For God is at work in you, both to will and to work for his good pleasure" (Phil. 2 : 13). Failure to understand this leads only to self-effort and consequent disillusionment. The positive side of surrender is found in the command, "Be filled with the Spirit" (Eph. 5 : 18). It is precisely this for which we ask now; *humbly beseeching thee, that all we, who are partakers of this holy Communion, may be fulfilled with thy grace and heavenly benediction*. We understand the word "fulfilled" in its original meaning, "filled full".

There is no merit whatever in our act of consecration. Sinners as we are, we are unworthy to offer any sacrifice. Yet it is our *bounden duty and service* to yield to God. He, in his mercy, accepts what we offer, *not weighing our merits, but pardoning our offences*. It is quite essential to recognise that even our highest actions are stained with sin. Our boldness in Christ must not blind us to our eternal unworthiness. All is *through Jesus Christ our Lord*. Through him we give honour and glory to God the Father; but also *with* him, because by faith we are united to him. And we offer praise *in the unity of the Holy Ghost*. The Holy Spirit is the bond of unity between the Father and the Son, and he unites us with Christ and with one another. This is one of the too few references in the service to the Holy Spirit, by whose operation Communion becomes a reality. As the Holy Trinity is eternal, so the honour and glory to the Three Persons in One God is *world without end*.

CHAPTER 20

THANKSGIVING

THE single directive, *Or this*, standing at the head of the second Post-Communion prayer, does not reveal anything of its history. In the first Prayer Book, this Prayer of Thanksgiving—with verbal differences—was the only prayer between the Communion and the Blessing. With the removal, in 1552, of the Prayer of Oblation to its present position, this 1549 composition became no more than an alternative. The pity is that we do not use them both. The Church of Ireland Prayer Book, which has so many things to commend it, has a rubric after the Lord's Prayer: "After shall be said *either or both* of the following Prayers." It is true that both contain the elements of thanksgiving and of consecration, but the approach is from two different angles.

Here the note of thanksgiving is uppermost. The first of the two long sentences which comprise the prayer is a kind of grace "for what we have received". It is no formal acknowledgment, but comes from the depth of our being: *we most heartily thank thee*. We thank God as those *who have duly received these holy mysteries*. The word "mysteries", which in the New Testament means truths which have been revealed by God, is here used to denote the bread and wine as the outward and visible sign of Christ's Body and Blood. In the same way the Prayer Book speaks of the water of Baptism being for the mystical (symbolical) washing away of sin. We have received the sacred symbols *duly*, with true repentance and living faith. Moreover we have sought to observe the divine Ordinance in the way our Lord commanded. We have, to the best of our ability and understanding, done what he told his Church to do. We can therefore thank him for what he has given.

First, *for that thou didst vouchsafe to feed us . . . with the spiritual food of the most precious Body and Blood of thy Son our Saviour Jesus Christ.* The meaning of the word "vouchsafe", as given in the Oxford *Dictionary*, is "condescend to grant". The same work points out that it is a combination of two words, "vouch" meaning "guarantee", and "safe" meaning "securely". We may surely read this literal meaning into the word in its present context. To those who *duly receive*, God *guarantees securely* to feed with Christ's Body and Blood. The Sacraments are not vague promises. They are "certain sure witnesses, and effectual signs of grace" (Article XXV).

ASSURANCE

Secondly, *and dost assure us thereby of thy favour and goodness towards us.* Very few go through life without any doubts about the goodness and love of God. The problem of evil, in some form or other, raises all kinds of questions. There is no final answer except in the Cross. And at the Lord's Table we are assured that Christ died for all, and that behind all the perplexities of life there is a God who loves each one of us, and cares with infinite concern for our destiny.

Thirdly, *and that we are ver(il)y members incorporate in the mystical body of thy Son, which is the blessed company of all faithful people.* The Holy Communion, duly received, assures us of our incorporation into Christ and his Church. It is not the Sacrament of incorporation: that is Baptism. The Lord's Supper *assures* us of our position in Christ, which is ours already by faith and Baptism. If we look at ourselves, our feelings, our behaviour, even our faith, we shall doubt whether we are Christians at all. In this Sacrament we have looked beyond ourselves to God, and what he has accomplished for us in Christ. Each communicant may know himself to be truly "a member of Christ, the child of God" (Catechism). Each is a *member* of Christ in the same sense that our hands, feet, eyes and ears are members of our body. We not only belong, we are part of him. We belong to his mystical Body, the Church, as distinguished from his natural Body. The Church, of which Christ is the head, is the blessed (or happy) company of all those who have faith in him. We cannot but be saddened that the essential unity of all Christian people has not yet brought us to kneel together at the one Table of the Lord.

Fourthly, *and are also heirs through hope of thy everlasting kingdom.* In one sense the kingdom of God has come already, when Christ came. But its full fruition awaits the consummation of all things at the Second Advent. So while the believer is already in the kingdom of God, "who calls you into his own kingdom and glory" (1 Thess. 2:12), he is also looking forward to inheriting the kingdom in the future. It is an *everlasting kingdom.* Says St. Paul: "In this hope we were saved. Now hope that is seen is not hope. For who hopes for what he sees? But if we hope for what we do not see, we wait for it with patience" (Rom. 8:24, 25). In the Holy Communion I receive the assurance that I have been made "a member of Christ, the child of God, *and an inheritor of the kingdom of God"* (Catechism). The Christian hope, no less than every other blessing, is ours *by the merits of the most precious death and passion of thy dear Son.* That is why true assurance is so very far removed from presumption.

OBEDIENCE

Now thanksgiving for all that God has given us must be followed by the offering of our lives. In this prayer we ask our heavenly Father *so to assist us with thy grace, that we may continue in that holy fellowship.* Even without specific mention of offering and presenting ourselves, our souls and bodies, that is what we are really doing. For we cannot continue in fellowship with the Lord and his people without whole-hearted commitment of our lives to him. And it is salutary to remember that we cannot live this life of obedience without the constant assistance of his grace.

The result of God's grace, working in us obedience, is that we may *do all such good works as thou hast prepared for us*

116 THE HOLY COMMUNION

to walk in. The New Testament will not for one moment coun-
tenance a doctrine of salvation which does not issue in good
works. "For we are his workmanship, created in Christ Jesus
for good works" (Eph. 2:10). But the Christian life is not a
frantic endeavour to do all the good works possible. There is an
orderliness and sense of direction in true service. We are to
do "good works, which God prepared beforehand, that we
should walk in them" (Eph. 2:10). It is an immense comfort to
know that God who prepares us for good works, is also preparing the particular good works for us to do. Guided service,
not hectic activity, is the mark of the dedicated Christian.

CHAPTER 21

THE END OF THE BANQUET

GLORIA IN EXCELSIS

WE come now to what is sometimes called the "Greater Doxology". It is a hymn dating from the fourth century, and was used at other services besides Holy Communion. In the first Prayer Book, as in the Sarum Missal before it, the *Gloria in Excelsis* came in the earlier part of the service as part of the preparation for Communion. The chief virtue in this would seem to be that any who were present at Ante-Communion only would have the opportunity for praise which is otherwise lacking. But the *Gloria* in its present place, where it has been since 1552, forms a grand climax to the offering of thanksgiving at the close of the service. It is a hymn, far more scriptural and worshipful than many modern hymns, and it is a pity that it is not always sung by the congregation standing, rather than said kneeling.

The opening sentence is taken directly from St. Luke's account of the Nativity, where in the Authorised Version we read: "Glory to God in the highest, and on earth peace, good will toward men" (Luke 2:14). The Revised Version has "peace among men in whom he is well pleased", and this is a truer translation of the Greek text. It is often assumed that a better version of the *Gloria* would be "on earth peace to men of good will". But as Neil and Willoughby say, "the meaning is the same, for it is not men of good will towards one another, but men who enjoy God's good will, or good pleasure, who are the promised recipients of peace".[1]

These opening words were the song of angels. We join in

[1] *The Tutorial Prayer Book*, p. 354.

117

their worship, but go on to use expressions which they could never use. In the words of a children's hymn, we have

> A song which even angels
>   Can never, never sing;
> They know not Christ as Saviour,
>   But worship him as King.

We who know him as Saviour worship with a gratitude and a humility of a different kind from that of the angels. True, in our adoration of the Father we praise, bless, worship, glorify, and give thanks for his great glory, but we know that we can only do this because of the redeeming work of Christ.

Here once again the alternating rhythm of our worship is seen. As the *Sanctus* is followed by the Prayer of Humble Access, so here the first paragraph of the *Gloria* is followed by the second. In our highest moments of devotion we need to remember that it is not in ourselves that we worship him. So we address God the Son, the Lamb of God, who takes away the sin of the world. Let him have mercy upon even our worship, which is stained with sin. The repetitive words *thou that takest away the sins of the world have mercy upon us* are not part of the original *Gloria in Excelsis*, but were introduced in the 1552 Prayer Book by mistake. They are omitted in the Scottish liturgy and in the newly revised Canadian Prayer Book. However, four centuries of use have made them a loved part of the liturgy adding to the earnestness of the plea. Let the same Saviour who has mercy upon us also receive our prayer. Let Christ, who not only died and rose again, but ascended and sits at the right hand of the Father, have mercy upon us.

Yet once more comes the *crescendo*. Humbly we have sought his mercy on our holy things. Now, forgetting ourselves entirely, we rise to great heights of adoring wonder: *For thou only art holy*. Certainly *we* are not. *Thou only art the Lord*. He has absolute right to the unconditional worship of our whole being. *Thou only, O Christ, with the Holy Ghost, art most high in the glory of God the Father*. This single reference to the Holy

Spirit seems to give too small a place to the Third Person of the Trinity. It is indeed true of the Holy Spirit that, as Jesus said: "He will glorify me, for he will take what is mine and declare it to you" (John 16:14). So even with only one reference to the Spirit, his work is still recognised in our worship of the Father, through the Son.

DEPART IN PEACE

"And when they had sung a hymn, they went out to the Mount of Olives" (Mark 14:26). At the close of the Passover Feast, during which he had instituted his Holy Supper, our Lord joined with the disciples in singing the Psalm which was traditional at that point. It was the conclusion of the Great Hallel (the six Psalms of praise beginning with Psalm 113). It must have been a wonderful experience, on that most solemn night, to hear him sing: "O give thanks unto the Lord, for he is gracious: because his mercy endureth for ever" (Ps. 118:1, Prayer Book Version). And then they went out to face all that was coming to them: the disciples to forsake him and flee, the Master to fight and win the supreme battle of all time. Psalm 118 well repays detailed study with that event in mind.

Our hymn has been the Greater Doxology, which in the American Prayer Book is closely associated with the Psalms, being permitted at the close of the last Psalm at Evening Prayer. We can see a close parallel between the Great Hallel at the Passover and the Greater Doxology at the Eucharist. In both cases it is the last great act of praise before going out to face whatever the world may have in store. As our Lord was always at peace, so may we be. The meaning of the Nunc Dimittis is often mistaken. It is not Simeon's prayer that he may die. He did not say, "Lord now *let* thy servant depart in peace." He said, "Lord, now *lettest thou* thy servant depart in peace." He was stating a fact: that God was allowing him to depart in peace now that he had seen his salvation. Simeon was very old, and certain to depart this life soon. The great point was that he could now depart *in peace*.

When we leave the church after Holy Communion it is with the expectation of *living* for God through the coming week. As Simeon rejoiced in God's peace for dying, so we are to know his peace for living. We hear of *the peace of God, which passeth all understanding.* The Blessing is spoken by *the Priest (or Bishop if he be present).* Like the Absolution, it is to come to us with the greatest possible authority of the principal Minister. Yet in the last analysis it is neither Bishop nor Priest who blesses, but the Lord himself.

The opening words of the Blessing are taken from Philippians 4:7, "And the peace of God, which passes all understanding, will keep your hearts and your minds in Christ Jesus." Note that it is God's own peace of which we are hearing. He is the "God of peace" (Phil. 4:9). He has peace in himself, always. That peace he is willing to impart to us. When we receive it, we find it to be beyond our understanding. It is not that it is unreasonable, but it transcends all our reasoning powers. This peace keeps, as a sentinel keeps guard before the castle gate, our hearts and minds. Intellect, will, emotion, all are kept from evil by the peace of God. And like every other blessing, it is "in Christ Jesus". So God's peace is to *keep your hearts and minds in the knowledge and love of God, and of his son Jesus Christ our Lord.* To know God is to love him, but we shall do neither until we have seen *his* love, revealed in Jesus Christ.

And the blessing of God Almighty, the Father, the Son and the Holy Ghost . . . It is well that there is no word "may" ("May the blessing . . .") for this only weakens the authoritative pronouncement. It is as if God *commands* his blessing on his waiting people. That blessing comes to us from the Father who loves us, the Son who redeemed us, the Holy Spirit who sanctifies us. It is not a blessing to be received only by individuals; it is to be *amongst you,* a corporate experience. And it is to *remain with you always.* To these words we say a fervent *Amen.*

PRACTICAL CONSIDERATIONS

At the end of the Holy Communion service are printed six Collects to be used when Ante-Communion is not followed by an administration of the Lord's Supper, or at other times. They do not form part of the service and so are not included for comment here.[1] They are sometimes called the Table Prayers, and are singularly beautiful.

The rubrics at the end of the service deal with matters which have mainly been discussed already in this book. A sentence about each paragraph will therefore suffice here. 1. This does not apply today, when there is Communion at least every Sunday and holy day. 2 and 3. The purpose of these rubrics is to make impossible the kind of "solitary Mass" which was one of the great abuses in the pre-Reformation Church. Discretion can be used in special circumstances. 4. It is clear that the clergy are expected to receive the Communion at least every Sunday, and many will wish to teach the laity the great benefit of doing the same. 5, 6, and 7. The matter of the bread and wine has already been dealt with.[2] The Priest is to eat and drink any of the consecrated Elements. This has a double purpose: it prevents irreverence on the one hand, and superstition on the other. 8. Besides directions that all should communicate at least three times a year, this paragraph is the legal basis for the custom of the Easter Offering. 9. The Minister and Church-wardens have the disposal of Communion Alms *only*, all other money collected being at the disposal of the Minister and the Parochial Church Council.

The final paragraph of the rubrics needs somewhat longer treatment. It is not really a rubric, since it is not "for the better direction of them that are to officiate in divine service". It is rather an official apology to meet the objections of those who thought that kneeling to receive Communion implied some

---

[1] See, however, in this series *The Collects*, by L. E. H. Stephens-Hodge.

[2] See page 57.

adoration of the bread and wine. Moreover, it was not printed in red (the word "rubric" comes from the Latin word *ruber*—red), but in black. It has become known as the Black Rubric. It states very clearly that *no Adoration is intended, or ought to be done, either unto the Sacramental Bread and Wine, there bodily received, or unto any Corporal Presence of Christ's natural Flesh and Blood*. This unequivocal teaching should be sufficient to allay any fear that kneeling suggests adoration of *the Sacramental Bread and Wine* which *remain still in their very natural substances, and therefore may not be adored; (for that were Idolatry, to be abhorred of all faithful Christians)*.

OUT INTO THE WORLD

Important as it may be to exclude error, as is done in the Black Rubric, it would be unhappy to end on a negative note, as if the Prayer Book were chiefly concerned with denying certain doctrines held by the Church before the Reformation. Kneeling was retained *for a signification of our humble and grateful acknowledgment of the benefits of Christ therein given to all worthy Receivers, and for the avoiding of such profanation and disorder in the holy Communion, as might otherwise ensue.* The conviction underlying everything that has been here written is that in the reverent use of the Prayer Book rite we have a true exposition of the Sacrament of our Redemption. That does not mean that there is not room for a wise revision of the Prayer Book, provided it remains true to biblical doctrine.

If all that we claim for the Holy Communion is true, what is to be the outcome of our regular participation? Faith is re-kindled, hope reawakened, love renewed. We rise from our knees with a new awareness of Christ who died for us, and who lives in us. But if it ends there, we have not held true communion with the God who so loved *the world*, the Christ who is the propitiation for the sins of *the whole world*, the Holy Spirit who creates the fellowship of *the world-wide Church*. We go forth from the Gospel Feast to proclaim Christ to the world. "For the divine blessing," writes Douglas Webster, "is always given at the point where the body of Christians, their worship completed, goes back into the world again. Perhaps this is why a famous bishop once said that for him the greatest moment in the Holy Communion was at the end, as he went out into the world with Christ."[1]

Every church building in which we have habitually worshipped for some time leaves its impress on our hearts and minds. This is outstandingly true of a church where we have grown up from early childhood, through the experience of adolescence and commitment to Christ, Confirmation and first Communion, growth in grace and vocation to a life's work. Such a church for the present writer is one where, over the chancel arch, were the words of the Great Invitation: "COME UNTO ME, ALL YE THAT LABOUR AND ARE HEAVY LADEN, AND I WILL GIVE YOU REST." Every worshipper could read and accept the invitation. Then, as the congregation turned to go out after the service, they were confronted with the Great Commission: "GO YE INTO ALL THE WORLD, AND PREACH THE GOSPEL TO EVERY CREATURE." Those two sayings of our Lord are an epitome of our experience as communicants. We come to him as worshippers for the provision of all our needs, but only in order that we may go with him as witnesses for the fulfilling of all his will.

[1] *Into All the World* (S.P.C.K.) p. 3.